Mama STORIES

Gifts From Our Mothers

Mama
STORIES

Gifts From Our Mothers

A breathtaking collection of stories by 13 dynamic daughters sharing their mothers through joy, pain, laughter, and resilience.

Edited by
ANGELA M. HAIGLER

Copyright © 2023 Angela M. Haigler All rights reserved.

No part of this book may be reproduced, distributed or transmitted in any form by any means, graphic, electronic, or mechanical, including photocopy, recording, taping, or by any information storage or retrieval system, without permission in writing from the author except in the case of reprints in the context of reviews, quotes, or references.

While the author has made every effort to ensure that the ideas, statistics, and information presented in this Book are accurate to the best of his/her abilities, any implications direct, derived, or perceived, should only be used at the reader's discretion. The author cannot be held responsible for any personal or commercial damage arising from communication, application, or misinterpretation of the information presented herein.

TITLE: Mama Stories
First Printed: 2023
Original Cover Art: © 2023 Mary Sanders
Cover Designer: Tomi Banks
Editor: Angela M. Haigler

ISBN: 978-1-959719-27-4
ISBN (eBook): 978-1-959719-26-7

Printed in the United States of America

Published by Victorious You Press™
Charlotte NC, USA

For details email joan@victoriousyoupress.com
or visit us at www.victoriousyoupress.com

Dedication

For my guardian angels:

My mother, Audrey Tobiclaire Haigler Kirven neé Robinson who was the inspiration for this collection. She left this earth two years before she could see the finished product.

My grandmother, Madeline White Robinson Harley. Her home was my haven and she always understood my heart.

My great-grandmother and namesake, Marguerite "Margaret" Thomas White Bennett. Her name is a flower and my middle name.

My Aunt "Big Frances" Thomas, who we called "Auntie." Though married to my great Uncle Wilbur, she always made me feel like one of her own.

My Aunt Lucille Coles, who always remembered my birthday. She provided McDonald's hamburgers for my Sweet 16th birthday party guests, because why couldn't she?

Acknowledgements

I'm grateful for the 2020 Cultural Vision Grant awarded to me by the Arts & Science Council. The grant provided matching funds which helped with the following:

- Securing additional instruction by award-winning essayists, Mary C. Curtis and Patrice Gopo
- Commissioning visual artist, Mary Sanders whose original artwork is used in the promotional pieces and in the cover art
- Contracting Tomi Banks who designed the promotional pieces and book cover

ABOUT THE MAMA STORIES WRITING PROJECT

The Mama Stories Writing Project established by Angela M. Haigler nurtures and celebrates the culture of Black women by shining the spotlight on an often unseen and unheard population: Black women over 40. The purpose of this project is to inspire emerging authors by providing educational support, an encouraging writing community and an opportunity for their stories to be seen and heard.

Contents

Introduction 1

Need You More Than Anything
by AMY COTTON 3

Woman to Woman
by KIRSTEN USSERY 13

Mother of Ones
by LUCY A. SAMS 21

Girl Forgotten
by TANNY SWAN 31

Love Celebrated, Nurturing Remembered
by TOMI BANKS 43

Mama Was Sanctuary
by RITA SAMUELS 51

Juanita's Gift
by MONICA BROWN NASH 65

My Girl
by TIFFANY GRANTHAM 75

Pass the Mic
by YAYA S. 85

Payback's a B*****!
by VESTA JOI.. 95

A Love Beyond Time and Space
by KANDACE GRANT 105

Taking Flight
by MARY SANDERS 117

Breathe
by ANGELA M. HAIGLER 123

About The Authors
.... 135

Introduction

A Gift: Something given willingly, usually without a price, where the giver often seeks nothing in return.

As children we were taught to accept a gift with gratitude, whether we liked it or not. Remember getting underwear for Christmas when you wanted a doll or truck? We were told to politely say thank you and keep our true feelings inside. We couldn't show our disappointment, these were gifts after all. "It's the thought that counts," we were told. Our mothers' gifts to us are similar.

Like the still popular game show, *Let's make a Deal*, we didn't know what was behind Door #2 if we chose it over the prize in front of us. But once the curtain flew open, the prize was ours to keep whether it was a check for $10,000 or a pack of ten t-shirts. Of course, we don't choose our mothers, however the feeling is similar. Over time we may choose to appreciate her gifts whether we hit the jackpot or not.

Our mothers are the ones whose absence or presence has a tremendous impact on our self-concept and well-being. They lay the foundation, provide the blueprint. It's a huge responsibility. Some mothers embrace everything about motherhood and give it their all. Others aren't up for the challenge; the gift of life is all they can do.

These stories reflect the wide range of gifts provided by mothers. These aren't stories about perfect women. These are stories of resilience, joy, laughter, and pain. These are stories by daughters who want their experiences shared. There is sure to be a story for everyone. These Mama Stories are our gift to you.

— Angela M. Haigler,
Editor and Director of The
Mama Stories Writing Project.

Need You More Than Anything

AMY COTTON

My mother stood five feet two inches tall with wavy, short, salt-and-pepper hair. She wore blue-tinted glasses that covered her dark brown eyes, and she had one black mole on her face. She always either had on tennis shoes or black pumps and what she lacked in height she made up for in the way she carried herself.

There she was, standing a few feet away from me talking to someone that I didn't recognize right away. She had a hearty voice that always commanded attention when she spoke, but it wasn't overbearing. Mama always had enough love to give not only to her children but to other people's children as well. Her hugs were always embraces with lots of warmth. Her loving arms gave me all the comfort I could ever need, her sweet perfume was a garden in the air as she hugged me.

"Open, open, open," I screamed at the top of my lungs, hoping that somebody could help me, but nobody came to my rescue. My body began walking down the narrow, dark green path, picking up the sound of people talking, yet no one said my name. My mouth opened, but nothing came out. It was as if my brain had been erased and had forgotten my

Mama Stories

name. There was a thick fog in the air that began to blind me. The only thing to do was lay down on the white clouds, drift off to sleep, and figure out where the noise was coming from.

Every attempt to open my eyes failed with the noise continuing to get louder and louder. Was someone trying to talk to me? Several voices were recognizable and then the clouds parted, and the heavenly gates opened with my Granny walking out in a long, white gown. With a puzzled look on my face, I just stood there, not taking one step forward or backward.

I began to fear for my life because my Granny died a long time ago and you only see people who have passed on when you're dead yourself. Nothing was making sense to me. I didn't know if I was dead or alive, but at that very moment I knew that Granny would be the key to all the answers formulating in my mind. The familiar, soft-spoken voice said, "Come!" With just that one word, my brown bare feet began moving slowly until our arms wrapped around each other for what seemed like an eternity because that was what it felt like. Finally, I looked up with tears flowing down my face, seeing a beautiful green garden full of red roses, white lilies, purple violets, yellow daisies, and every flower known to mankind. Soft violin music played in the background, pleasing to my ears.

The green pasture in the garden created a seat for us to sit on and we began talking but neither of us opened our mouths. I looked around, expecting to see more people around us due to hearing other voices around us earlier, but it was just the two of us.

It was at that moment Granny began to answer all my questions without saying a word, but through our minds. The first thing she told me was that I wasn't dead. It never occurred to me to ask her what had happened to me and why my body was in heaven. I didn't want to ruin the special moment of spending time with her. She had been dead since I was ten years old. She immediately let me know it wasn't a social visit and she had lots of detailed information that had to be told right away. Her eyes had a sparkle that lit up in the sky and she began talking about the night she met with the death angel and that she wasn't mad at my mama at all.

Suddenly, there was a loud beeping noise, and I could hear someone saying, "I'll turn it off. I got to take her blood anyway. Amy, can you hear me?" It was like my body had been floating in outer space and was returning to Earth. I still couldn't tell where I was or who was talking to me. As my head began to turn to where the voice was coming from, Granny's beautiful silky bronze face faded far away into the clouds.

No longer able to see the garden, my body drifted back into a long, deep sleep. Occasionally I heard the voices of people who seemed nearby coming closer, then fading away. I had no way to tell if we would ever meet in human form.

There were days when my spirit could feel people in the room, but I couldn't understand why there was sadness in their voices. They always said they would be back. Couldn't they take me with them? Suddenly, like turning on a light switch, I could feel my Mama combing my hair, but where was she standing? I must be dreaming because Mama lives in Indiana and hadn't combed my hair since I was eleven years old. Yet, for some reason, I couldn't shake the feeling. As the voices grew louder, I kept hoping my eyes would suddenly open. Everything was a blur and things only cleared up a tiny bit, but just enough. A child knows the sound of her mother's voice.

It was as if my body had been split into two people--one person who was aware of what was going on (because pieces of the conversation were becoming very vivid), and the other person who was not aware of anything--in a deep coma, sleeping away her life. Not once did she awaken to greet her guests in their conversation, or even know that she had guests.

"I need a bigger comb, do you have a stronger shampoo that I can use on her hair?" My mother's voice.

"No, this is what I have personally on me that you can use!" Another voice, maybe the nurse?

Flash Forward

Every morning, Mama got up, came into my room, and asked me what I wanted for breakfast. Then she would go down to the kitchen to make her coffee as she had already picked out my clothes for the day. For several days she had been talking about how she missed her house, her dog (Winston), the girls (Angela and Donya), and her church family. Whenever she brought up the subject, I tried to convince her to move them all down by me so we could be closer.

One night when she was showing me how to make fried chicken for dinner, she blurted out that my brother Erskine would be arriving to take her home and that she would be leaving in a few days. I immediately began yelling as if someone had ripped out my heart. "No Mama, please don't leave me! Please stay here! I need you more than anything!"

She looked me in the eyes and said, "Amy, stop this noise. You're too old for this. I've been with you since May and it's time for me to go home and for you to stand on your own."

I knew the day would come when Mama would feel the need to go back to Indiana, but I just wasn't ready for her to leave at that moment. My mind went into total depression, and I felt each breath would be my last. I wanted to die. Who would be there in the morning to eat breakfast with me? It had been Mama who picked out my clothes and taught me how to plan my day so that I just wouldn't sit around being bored. It was Mama who rode the bus with me to my appointments or greeted me at the door when I got back home. It had been her words of wisdom that helped me see that I was more than what I thought I was on the days I felt like giving up.

The first time Mama prepared to leave me, right before school began, I didn't want her to leave, but I knew she was getting homesick, and I knew I didn't want to live in Indiana. Earlier in June before my husband Curtis went back out of town for work, Mama let him know that she would be taking us to Anderson, our hometown. Part of me wanted to see Daddy. We talked every day on the phone, but the other part of me didn't want to go. The home where I was at the time still seemed like a foreign place. I left the hospital and visited a two-bedroom brick townhouse where nothing looked familiar. I was too afraid to go upstairs. I slept on one couch, Curtis slept on the other couch, and Mama stayed upstairs. My anxiety shot through the roof thinking about traveling to see another home, even if it was Mama's.

We didn't have the best adventure traveling there and got into our first fight at my godparents' house in Ohio. It had started to get dark and they asked to get a hotel but decided not to. Then it got pitch black outside and all I could see was darkness (like when I first walked to the car and things went blank). Oh, how I hated that feeling of not knowing where I was going, just walking endlessly in the night, waiting for someone to jump out and scare me with their voice.

I pitched a big fit. Mama said I was acting like a two-year-old; and maybe I was. At the time I didn't feel like it, I just felt a wave of emotions come over me and like the students I teach, I couldn't express my feelings very well. My godparents tried to calm us all down so that we could get home. My son even took off, walking in the dark due to all the yelling and fussing that was happening.

Everything was going way too fast. I tried to call Curtis to come get me, but he wasn't picking up. Mama finally told me to shut up and don't say anything else until we got home. Home? Where was that? What was the saying, "There's no place like home?" Yet no place felt like home! When the white garage door went up at two in the morning, everyone piled out of the black Saturn Vue and began unloading the van. There was one person not moving. Me! After a few minutes, Mama came out the door attached to the garage demanding that I get out and come into the house.

Walking into the house, I saw that it was decorated all in blue, silver and white. There were pictures all over the walls. Mama kept asking me, "Do you know who that is?"

"No," was the answer that continued to flow out of my mouth over and over.

The room kept spinning around and around in a circle while I just stood on the blue carpet until my feet began to hurt and I wanted to sleep with the one person that I brought into this world, my son. At that time, I just wanted to feel safe and secure. I wanted to stop feeling alone with nobody understanding my true feelings. After a few minutes, I went into Mama's room and sat on her queen-sized bed that was over forty years old and was still in great condition. The 100 percent cotton comforter on the bed was neatly pulled back with several big pillows decorating its top with smaller pillows thrown to the side making room for the both of us to sleep for the night.

We sat up for hours talking about my fear of the dark and why it freaked me out so badly when Angela wouldn't stop for the night. For the first time that night, Mama's harsh tone became gentle and soft-spoken. It was that same gentle voice attached to that sturdy, small body that stood in front of the deep fryer, pulling out pieces of crispy, golden-fried chicken and laying them on the plate. It was there that I could see her lips moving but no longer allowed my ears to bear witness to what was coming out because I could only focus on one word, "Leaving!" That one word stuck in the back of my throat making me choke up every time it came to mind. See, Mama had become more than just my mother. She became my best friend, the one who tells me what I need to hear when I don't want to hear it.

Mama Stories

When I would say, "Why me? Why did I have to have a stroke?" Mama would come back with, "Why not you? What makes you so different from others?" She left me with that wisdom to ponder and she never allowed me to throw a pity party.

Eventually, I came back from my sadness patrol, and although I had a better appreciation of how far I had come, I still couldn't stomach the fact that she couldn't see I wasn't ready. I left the kitchen, flinging myself on the worn, green couch, stating that I couldn't do it without her by my side. I thought she'd follow me into the room and change her mind. Instead, she yelled at me to get back into the kitchen and finish frying the chicken.

We laugh now at the thought of her not following me and forcing me to finish cooking dinner. The days flew by so fast and finally, that big day came when my brother, Erskine, was ready to head back home. Standing in front of my doorway, holding onto Mama as we gave our last hugs, kisses, and goodbyes, it felt like I was losing my only friend forever. Mama kept telling me, "Stop crying, Amy. You're going to be okay." Then Erskine drove off with my best friend, leaving me to figure out everything on my own.

That first day, waking up on my own without seeing her beautiful smile first thing in the morning stung. No longer could I look out my door and see her in one of her vibrant, colorful robes. Talking would now be limited to over the phone. Every time we talked, she would always say, "Now, you remember what I told you about this or that?" Those words allowed me to get through the roughest part of this journey. Once I got lost on the bus, came out too late and my Lyft left me. Another time I was at the store, struggling to figure out what I was supposed to purchase. I knew

Mama was just a phone call away and would do her best to help me, even from a distance.

Today, I owe my life to my son Ty and Mama. Mama sacrificed everything: the comfort of her bed, her dog, her appointments, her life. She gave it up and I know it wasn't easy, but she did all of that to help her baby get better.

Black mamas have a saying, "I brought you into this world and I'll take you out." In my case, I was on my way out and Mama brought me back in. She wouldn't let me give up, not one day. She taught me how to be a fighter, how to strengthen my faith in Christ, and how to embrace my new purpose in life.

Every time I asked her how she was doing; her reply was always "Wonderful!" I felt her powerful energy coming through the phone. Mama taught me that everyone has a story. She gave me the words I live by every day, "When you're complaining about your situation, wishing you were in someone else's shoes, someone else could be wishing they were in your shoes."

God wasn't ready for me on that day, my Granny told me so in the beautiful garden. I survived a stroke, was loved back to life, and nudged out of the nest to reclaim my independence. Sometimes I stumble, but most days I succeed. I thank Mama for her role in my continued victory. This is my love letter to her.

Woman To Woman

KIRSTEN USSERY

My mom is an early riser. While I'm still emerging from sleep at 10 a.m., she has already worked out, read the bible, and tucked her bed up so tight that you'd hardly know it had been slept in. By noon, when I'm finally mentally prepared for a conversation, my mom is fully dressed, eating breakfast and sipping coffee. If she has a cake or cookies to bake, the intoxicating aroma of butter, lemon, cinnamon, or chocolate is lingering in the air as early as 10 in the morning.

On one day, my mom sat at her small kitchen table in the basement apartment looking down at her fidgeting hands. We'd been arguing and then not speaking for most of the day, and she had threatened to leave. To this day, neither of us remembers the reason for the disagreement, but I'm sure it had something to do with her treating me like a child. My nearly forty years of life still had not earned me exemption from her instruction or warnings. I'd been on my own at that point for nearly twenty-two years, a few years more than the eighteen I'd lived under her roof. However, in the gap of time we were apart, she hadn't seen all the situations I'd navigated without her instruction. She wanted to catch up on the lessons she'd been unable to teach me while I was adulting, like how to properly clean a pan, how to drive, and the pros and cons of procrastination. For the life of me, I still don't know where that sweet girl she refers to so often went. I think I lost her in my thirties along with my childhood fantasies of becoming a rich novelist with at least two children by forty.

I'd come down to apologize for my part in the argument to find her seated at the small glass table, vegan recipes and health books underneath, with the TV blaring. I'd renovated the basement space with laborious detail just for her. The walls were a warm shade of sand with a red accent wall to match the red loveseat she'd picked out. Although it wasn't enough room for all her things, she'd adorned the walls and windowsills with family photos, lighthouses, and other knick-knacks she'd collected over the years. I had a small kitchenette installed so she wouldn't have to come upstairs to cook if she didn't want to. The custom closet was packed with clothes and shoes, and there were still more stored in totes and boxes in the unfinished laundry area.

It wasn't lavish and I knew it didn't compare to the house she'd left behind that was all hers, but it was cozy and comfortable, and she'd made it her home. It was all a part of the promise I'd made to convince her to move from her small hometown of Hickory, North Carolina (population 40,000) to the large metropolitan city of Detroit, Michigan (population around 700,000) to live with me. I promised she'd have her own space, her own income from baking cakes for my new vegan restaurant, and that we'd be able to find a nearby church community for her. She was able to drive my old Toyota to the church two blocks away, and she drove the back streets to her yoga lessons a few miles away. I assumed with these things in place, she'd be just as independent as she was back home. I thought she had everything she needed to create an amazing new life alongside the one I'd spent the past decade creating while we'd lived apart. I didn't realize the gravity of the adjustment she'd have to make, nor did I realize how reliant on me she'd be in a big, new city. Until that point, my perception of my mom was that she was larger than life. To me, she possessed the strength to topple any man who stood in her way, freeze a wrongdoer with one side eye, and trample any life obstacle with her shield of strength.

I remember looking up at her when I was a girl, her 5'3" stature towering over me. No one was as strong or beautiful as my mom. Her skin was the perfect shade of caramel, and her lips were in perfect contrast to my own full ones that had garnered so much ridicule in my past. She didn't seem to have any problems finding a man to love her. Once, when my mom told a man she didn't want to see him anymore, he hit his head against the wall until his face turned red. When a man was out of line or not pulling his weight, she let him know.

"If I cussed them out, trust and believe they needed it, they deserved it...I probably didn't cuss them out enough," she said to me recently and we both burst into laughter.

My first stepfather was drunk one day and thought he was going to raise a hand to my mom. Before I could react, she'd knocked him to the ground and kicked him out of the house with her small but strong feet. I couldn't help but feel a little sorry for him and when my mom saw that, she sent me to my room. I learned that no matter what, I was to have her back.

Mama Stories

She never missed a day of work, and my needs were never unmet. My mom was always there--unlike the mothers of those girls I always admired growing up who, at very young ages, had the freedom to go wherever and do whatever they wanted. As an adult, I came to understand the consequences those mothers paid for allowing those freedoms. It was made evident by the different ways our lives turned out.

I learned a lot when my mom moved to Detroit. She'd been strong and fearless in raising me, and the image I'd held of her as this superwoman had influenced my entire life. It pushed me to get through college when I felt overwhelmed juggling sports and academics. It pushed me through my corporate climb to becoming an entrepreneur when I felt unsure of myself. I learned, from watching my mom over the years, that the only way to achieve is to work hard even when situations grow tough.

That image pushed me through the struggles of relationships because I wanted what she seemed to be always striving for, a partner, a home, a family. And even when those relationships weren't always good for me, I tried to make things work, so I could become the next level of strong woman, a 2.0 version of my mom. But after my mom came to live with me, I learned that she was far more complicated than the one-dimensional caricature of her I had created in my mind. Somehow, she was both fearless and fearful. She was strong enough to raise a daughter alone, brave enough to move over 600 miles, leaving everything she knew of her life behind, and independent enough to break the mold of everyone in our family to become a vegan yogi. At the same time, she was afraid to drive on the freeway by herself, unwilling to figure out technology without my assistance, and unable to introduce herself to anyone new without my help.

One day while I was working in the restaurant, my mom called crying and hysterical. She intended to visit the Riverwalk after yoga class but somehow got lost, made the wrong turn, and was almost on her way to Canada via the tunnel. I raced out to find her only five miles down the road in a gas station parking lot two blocks from her intended destination. After that day, I couldn't get her to drive anywhere beyond a few miles of the house and she was too terrified to try taking the main roads.

As I sat in the basement apartment across from my mother, I didn't recognize the woman in front of me. She could always say a thousand words with one look, but vulnerability was a look I can't recall ever seeing on her face before that moment.

"You're all I have. I don't have anyone else," she said through her tears. It was so foreign to me, seeing her cry, that I wasn't sure it was really happening. I reviewed my mind's reels trying to remember if I'd ever seen her cry before. I'm sure she cried at my grandmother's funeral, but I don't remember witnessing any tears. I remember her being very quiet and calm. It took a couple of seconds for my mind to catch up to the moment and get the message. She was really crying.

The woman who raised me single-handedly, protected me better than many moms were able to do for their daughters, put the fear of God in me with one look, was telling me she felt dependent on me. That was probably one of the hardest things she'd done in her life. I didn't realize the emotional toll all the change had brought on her and it never occurred to me that I was her only emotional lifeline. I'd intended to lift the financial burden from her by having her live with me, but I had no idea the emotional burden we'd both take on by living and learning together, mother and daughter, as two adult women. And yet, it would take more years of us living together and a pandemic forcing us to confront one another daily for me to finally accept my mom for the complex woman she is and for her to also accept me as a woman, no longer the little girl gripping her torso, afraid to face the world.

Due to a perfect storm of happenings, we moved back to Charlotte. When the pandemic began, we were living with my aunt. It was only supposed to be for a couple of months (to allow time to find the right place), but thanks to COVID, we ended up staying with my aunt for eight months. My mom remained glued to the television every day—all day. She didn't miss a new development and she made it her personal mission to ensure my aunt and I took all the COVID precautions. Her drills for cleaning outside products before bringing them inside the house along with her strict enforcement of the no-contact policy left me full of anxiety.

She wasn't satisfied with knowing we knew the rules, she only felt safe if we'd heard them from her first. It was like having a mirror reveal to me the worst parts of myself. I came to understand the origin of why I felt a need to control things that can't be controlled in my life. In all those years I lived away from home, building my career, getting married and divorced, and starting a business, my mom still felt like protecting me meant making sure I knew the rules of engagement from her; otherwise, I would surely catch COVID or get into a car accident resulting from texting and driving.

Because they do such a good job at shielding their pain and frailties from us as girls, we may have grown up thinking our mothers were super-human creatures who could withstand anything. After we become women, it may take a while for some of us to make the connection that the abuses we suffered and our struggles with significant others and jobs are the same ones our mothers suffered before us. My mom was not always in the mood to talk about the past, but being stuck in the house with her for an entire year, although frustrating, has also been a blessing. We were able to talk about her life before me and about my life. I only wish I'd had the courage to have had those conversations with her earlier.

The years my mom lived with me in Detroit were some of the hardest in my life. Not only did I feel responsible for her adjustment and happiness after her move, but my marriage was falling apart. Although I'm sure it was difficult for my mom to hear the ugly words being tossed back and forth, and I'm sure she sometimes felt stuck in the middle, she never interfered. However, once my ex and I separated and it was clear we would not reconcile and I fell into a deep depression for months, my mom finally broke her silence.

"You are a strong woman! Don't let anyone make you feel less than. Get up and get yourself together," she said, though in far more elegant words than that.

She shared with me that it wasn't easy for her when her marriage to my last stepfather failed. She'd wanted it to work, and she felt alone for a while, but those feelings were only temporary. She had many moments in her life when she didn't quite know what her next step would be. She didn't always have a plan and sometimes life

Mama Stories

derailed the plan she put in place, but she pushed through. She let me know I was made of the same stuff she was made of.

I would push through too, no matter how much it hurt. To her, *I* was the superwoman. I was incredibly smart and brave. I moved away from home and made so much happen for myself without the help of anyone. She was amazed at what I'd achieved and said I had the power to create whatever I wanted, and no one could take away my strengths. I never knew my mom felt that way about me.

She was right. I am strong and I survived. I'm grateful that although time and distance separated us for many years, she's with me now and I can get these insights from her. Yes, she still treats me like a child sometimes and it is very annoying, but her support has kept me strong and humble. No, she didn't pass down any superhuman strength or powers to me, she passed down womanly wisdom and acute insights that helped shore up my self-perception. I guess those are the best superpowers any woman could receive from her mother.

Mother Of Ones

LUCY A. SAMS

Lana smiled easily as she watched the children scoop the small granules of sand into the shovel. Jabril and Trinity loved the park and Lana enjoyed seeing her children smile. She settled into her seat on the faded green park bench. Tilting her head towards the sun, she grabbed the latest magazine featuring her Mommy Mentor, Oracene, who she affectionately called "Lady O." The article didn't disappoint. Lana loved the sapphire blue tailored suit Lady O wore. Her daughters looked lovely too. They wore gold tulle ball gowns and gold sneakers as they stood confidently holding their latest trophies. Lady O had done an amazing job raising "winners" despite the sexism and bigotry her girls often faced from dominating in a predominantly white sport.

Lana truly admired Lady O's grace and class in such hostile territory. Lana's own mother, Maxine, was a force to be reckoned with when it came to advocating for and protecting her children. Maxine's approach was more "in your face" and had the potential to get physical if need be. Her five-foot-nothing stature and easy smile were the versions most people received. Many victims could tell you from first-hand accounts that Maxine "did not play" about her kids.

Mama Stories

In public or in private, any injustice to young Lana and her siblings would be dealt with immediately. Since becoming a parent, Lana had struggled finding her own balance and defining her way as a mother.

She turned the page to an image of Lady O leaning against the column of an international stadium as her two girls casually linked arms. They appeared to be happily climbing the steep concrete steps to join Lady O as she led the way. Oracene navigated spaces that weren't always welcoming to her children with such regality. Lana could relate. Her own neighborhood had few people that looked like her, but the educational resources and opportunities were plentiful and would benefit her young children in the coming years. She flipped to the final page of the feature and she heard Jabril cry, "Mommy! Mommy!" She jumped up and rushed to his side in the sandbox. Jabril looked up at her, blinking and crying with a trail of sand from his cheek to his eye. Lana tried to calm him as she fumbled with the zipper on the fanny pack she often wore. The first aid kit was inside. Jabril had finally stopped clawing his eyeball.

"How much do you charge?" Lana looked up into the round blue eyes and pinched, inquisitive face of a petite white woman. Her brown bob framed her face perfectly, the bangs emphasizing her furrowed brow that remained scrunched as she waited for a reply. Her arms rested against a mint green stroller.

"Excuse me?" Lana responded, looking around and wondering if the unfamiliar woman was speaking to her.

"You are so good with the children. What is your hourly rate?" the woman asked.

Mother of Ones

Lana's hands trembled slightly as the realization set in that the woman assumed she was a nanny. She felt the blood rising from her diaphragm to her temples and tried to calm herself. Was it an honest mistake? Sure, she was younger than most everyone else in her neighborhood. Yes, her style of dress was youthful, not frumpy. Should she be offended?

What would Maxine do? Lana's Mama would tell Miss Brown Bob off in such a "head-to-toe" way that the woman's face would be red for days. But what would Lady O do? Just as Lana parted her lips to reply, Jabril tugged on her sleeve. "Mommy, my eyeball hurts," he whimpered. Miss Brown Bob's face went from startled to embarrassed within milliseconds. She whipped her stroller around and scurried up the path without another word. Lana turned to her injured child and made a show of inspecting his eyeball for any last specks of sand, as her trembling hands kept busy. She tilted her head up to feel the sun, but it didn't feel as warm.

"Time to go my loves," she called to Jabril and Trinity as she walked towards the faded green bench to retrieve her glossy new magazine.

"Aunt Lana, can I have the chocolate too?" Asia asked excitedly, trying to remove her hand from her aunt's grasp while reaching for the orange wrapper. To her left, Lana could see Jabril grab and put down small packages of jellybeans. Trinity stood on the other side, waiting and watching her little cousin's efforts to free Lana's grip.

"Just one second Asia. Let me see how much the gas will cost first."

"But Aunt Lana, I really, really need this chocolate. Can I have it? Huh? Huh? Huh?"

"Ugh, I can't stand that type of child," remarked the woman in line behind them. Lana turned quickly, assessing the woman from head to toe, starting with her freshly moussed gray strands to her meticulously folded navy socks.

"What type of child?" Lana asked, locking eyes with the woman.

"You know, *those* types," stated the woman before glancing away. Asia immediately stopped whining. She had never seen her aunt raise her voice to a stranger. Jabril walked up on the scene, not noticing what had just occurred. He held a carefully selected bag of small orange and yellow speckled jellybeans.

"Mom, can..." The words died on his lips as Lana held up her hand, crossing guard style. She gave the woman her full attention.

"Lady, are you off your meds? You must be crazy to ever say anything about someone else's child."

The woman's face turned beet red. The cashier gave a nervous chuckle. The entire store felt frozen in that single moment. What would Maxine do? Slap the woman across the face and wait for the police. What would Oracene do? Call the media using the speed dial feature on her cellphone.

Lana felt the anger rising to her temples, making her ears burn.

I can't go to jail! Who would pick up the kids from this gas station?

Her decided form of retaliation turned out to be more meticulous, calculating, and intentional. She walked out, snapped a picture of the license plate of the woman's light gray SUV, and drove away.

"Time for the park," Lana announced to a car full of children. "Yeah!!" they responded.

Later that evening, Lana pulled out the chair to her desk and turned on her computer. Navigating to the State Department of Motor Vehicles web page, she located the inspections and violations section, pulled out her cell phone and pulled up the image she had taken earlier of the woman's SUV. Using terms she heard her husband, a mechanic, use while describing a vehicle that couldn't pass inspection, she typed in the license plate number and searched for any violations which may have been associated with that vehicle. She copied the plate number to several more fields before hitting enter; deleted the picture, then joined her family in the living room for movie night.

"Who wants popcorn?" she asked in the sing-song way her family had become accustomed to. Mission accomplished.

The extra lesson appeared to be paying off. Jabril's fencing matches seemed like light work lately. Lana was beginning to run out of space for his trophies on the mantle. Tournament days were long, but Lana came fully prepared with her latest knitting project and snacks. Jabril appeared to be a bit nervous as his name got added to the next bracket. This would be the last match of the day. Jabril and Hank had been friends since pre-K. In fact, Lana had told Emily, Hank's mom, about how much Jabril enjoyed fencing, so she decided to sign Hank up.

On this one day, Jabril and Hank were matched up as opponents. They sized each other up in a shadow dance that appeared both elegant and deadly. Their foils were drawn, stating their lethal intent as the minutes ticked by. The masks meant to protect their faces also concealed their emotions. Lana chewed her jaw and Emily nibbled her jagged cuticles as their sons maintained their poise in the piste. Jabril toyed with Hank much longer than his other opponents, but ultimately put him out of his misery. As the director announced Jabril's victory in the final bout, Hank removed his mask revealing a face wet with tears. He scanned the crowd and locked in on his mother. Her apparent surprise resulted in a sound loud enough for Lana to hear. Then she gathered her things and made her way to her wounded cub. Lana zipped her tote and headed in the opposite direction to meet Jabril.

"Congratulations Champ!" Lana shouted as she saluted her son. He glanced up and gave her an easy smile.

"Thanks, Mom," he said.

"Next stop, Misty Stables to check out your sister. Let me call your dad and see if they need us to bring lunch."

Jabril adjusted the strap of his equipment bag and followed Lana to the beige Prius.

"Wet wipes and a change of clothes are in the back," she told her son as he scrambled into the backseat, and she glided in on the driver's side. LaDarius met them in the parking lot.

"Thanks for lunch, Babe. Jabril and I will probably head to the house after we run a few errands." Lana stepped outside the car, exchanged car keys with her husband and gave him a quick peck on the lips as she grabbed Trinity's lunch.

Lana made her way towards the arena. The silhouette of the stable cast a shadow over the arena as the sun began to go down. Trinity sat erect on the chestnut gelding. As he galloped past, Lana held her breath. Trinity tightened her hands on the reigns and halted. Once the dust settled, Lana took a tentative glance at the three pale faces that scribbled fervently on hidden pieces of paper. Trinity sat atop the massive horse as sweat escaped the confines of her helmet. Her face pensive, she awaited the judges' verdict. Would they deem her a competent rider? Trinity Steele, third place! Lana glanced over as Trinity made her way out of the arena at an even clip. Lana prayed Trinity was happy about her result. One never knew what was fair or not at events where you were the *only one*. Lana gathered her denim jacket and went to join her daughter, greeting her with a packaged smile and kudos for reigning in a massive beast.

"Hey Mom. Did you see me? I kept my heels flat this time and tightened up on the reigns like Ms. Julia said I should." Trinity often replayed each event to find flaws. Her goal was to always be the best, and she believed anything less than first place was a loss. Lana kept it light and just listened as Trinity recalled the morning events Lana had missed due to Jabril's competition.

One event complete, thought Lana. Two more days full of questioning stares and feigned indifference. Your daughter rides horses? "Yes, she does," Lana would answer for the eightieth time as the Karens and Beckys smirked, made small talk, and gifted her with smiles that never reached their eyes.

"Hi Lana. Have you been by the concession stand yet? They have the sign-up sheet for Farm Day. We would love it if you could join us," said Mary as she peered into Lana's eyes. Lana took a step back. Mary often stood too close to people while talking. The middle-aged woman's faded hair resembled the tail of a mare, mangled and dull. Mary always wore leggings and cowboy boots, and that day was no different. Her denim shirt, knotted on her right hip, emphasized the challenge Mary's leggings had to encompass the girth of her thighs. Her worn, faded brown boots, were covered in red clay.

Lana cleared her throat and gave Mary her best smile. "Mary, you know LaDarius and I work long hours which makes it difficult for us to volunteer compared to the other families at Misty Stable." Lana looked for Mary's reaction. Observing just a nod, she continued "I can definitely donate some money to get refreshments for the volunteers for Farm Day."

"That won't be necessary. The riders have an endowment that covers those types of expenses. Maybe your family will be free in the fall if the Farm Day date is available earlier."

"The last quarter of the year we often save our time-off to enjoy the holidays together as a family. I'd be more than happy to volunteer at the concession stand for one of the upcoming shows if you still need some help."

"We would definitely appreciate that." Mary peeled her thin, cracked lips into a brief smile, then walked away. Both women knew Lana's offer to man the concession stand was insincere and not possible. Concession stand opportunities filled up fast. In fact, there was a six-month waiting list.

Lana pulled her phone out of the front pocket of her denim jacket and shot a quick text to LaDarius. The emoji she chose showed the head of a bull and a mound of soil. LaDarius knew what that meant. The two of them had already agreed that those people would never see them break a sweat. Between the money they shelled out for Trinity's ride time and private lessons, and the constant uniform add-ons needed as she progressed, they flat out refused to volunteer for any tasks that made them feel like they were working on a plantation.

Still glancing at her phone, Lana headed towards the arena. As she turned the corner, she heard a commotion. Sierra, the wildest horse at the stable, was whinnying and rearing. Mia, the stable owner's daughter, cussed at the horse as she attempted to get her in a stall. Trinity ran up and calmed Sierra. Like a young horse whisperer, she guided the mare into the stall in a matter of minutes. Instead of offering thanks, Mia chastised Trinity for not being on deck for her next event. Lana lowered her phone and began a slow, deliberate stroll toward the two, noting the disrespect leveled at her daughter. She hoped the measured pace would help calm her exploding emotions.

Brenda, the stable owner was a passionate instructor who made each rider feel welcome. Mia was the opposite. Mia was miserable and lashed out at many of the young riders with a fury that extended beyond the offense. Trinity had never brought home any horror stories about Mia nor had Lana witnessed anything directed toward her daughter until that day.

"Why don't any of you ever listen?" Mia shouted as Lana approached. Lana's hands trembled as she saw her daughter's eyes start to water. Trinity locked eyes with her mother causing Mia to turn to see exactly what Trinity was looking at. Mia turned completely around to face Lana whose face was still crimson with rage. "I was just letting Trinity know..." Mia started.

Lana held up her hand. In a voice barely above a whisper said, "Not a soul on this earth talks to my child like that. You are not safe right now. Go and get your mother immediately."

Mia took a step back before scurrying away. Lana reached for her child just as the first tears fell from Trinity's eyes. "Mama's here," Lana said as she held her child in the tightest embrace and waited for Brenda. This time she didn't need advice from Maxine or Lady O. She knew exactly what to do.

Girl Forgotten

TANNY SWAN

To this day, there's one song by The Isley Brothers I avoid. It's the slow, rhythmic tune belted by one of the most successful Black R&B bands of the 1970s. Last week, while driving on Highway 1 from Santa Cruz to San Francisco, the song assaulted my Spotify playlist. I hate it when that happens. I really want to know who gave Spotify the right to randomly select songs solely based on my listening history. I really think there should be some type of general warning: *I'm about to play (insert traumatic song here). Is that okay? If I play this song, will it send you straight to your therapist's couch? Or will a few shots of tequila dull the pain you'll feel once the memories swallow you whole?*

My first instinct was to immediately skip forward to the next song, but I didn't. Instead, with the salty, warm breeze flying into my rented car windows, I surrendered.

Can I go on... my way... without you?

I let the song play. Loud. I even turned it up. Louder. The Isley Brothers held me captive until the last few seconds until I had no

Mama Stories

other choice but to pull to the side of the road, weeping uncontrollably with the Pacific Ocean lapping peacefully a few feet away. Violent, conflicting emotions pulled me into scattered, hidden memories.

It was 1975, and I was standing in the living room of my cousin's house in Michigan. It took me a long time to fully understand how I was related to them, but it didn't matter to my younger self. They were family, people to call my own besides my mother. I must have been about five years old, and my mother was resting in the darkened bedroom to the left of the living room. She had a gigantic afro and someone had just told me to let her rest. She was lying in the bed, her bright skin glowing. She did not look physically sick to me at all, but all the grown-ups around me seemed to know differently.

"Tanny, baby, close the bedroom door and let your mama rest."

The room was quiet, except for the AM radio humming in the corner. *I'll Always Come Back to You* filled the room with its solemn tempo. I wish I could recall what happened next. I was five, the age when most people can find their earliest memories in the recesses of their minds. But I can't. I rarely remember anything more than what I've written here. Truthfully, I have no reason to doubt the people who are my storytellers, so I cling to every recollection of little me.

"You were a quiet child."

"So sweet."

"You stayed under your mother most of the time."

Girl Forgotten

My mother was a beautiful young woman. Her high school black and white portrait perfectly captured her smooth, vanilla complexion and deep, magnetic eyes. Most of us can identify at least one thing about ourselves we dislike. For me, it's my forehead, yielding an inch more than I really would like it to. For my mom, it's her first name. While pregnant with my second daughter, I asked my mom how she felt about her first name becoming my daughter's middle name. Her face twisted into a squished frown, frustrating me as she nonchalantly dismissed something about her that I loved so much. Was her name, given to her by her own mother, too plain? Too black? Too white? Too urban?

"I don't know," she repeated. "Seems like everyone I knew growing up was named Pat."

I now know that my own intentional self-affirmations are an integral part of my heightened need to validate my self-worth. The older I become, the more I see the reflection of my mother, beautiful, strong, resilient, proud. We have the same soft, round cheeks and tender eyes. I wish my mother could see herself through my lenses. I try to remind her that she is the most beautiful person in the world.

Throughout the years, I have heard people call her Pat. Patty Ann. Patricia Ann. Then there's my personal favorite, which I assume she self-assigned: *Pattai*. With an accent on the second "a." A few weeks ago, while flipping through her crate of phonograph jazz albums, I saw that sassy name written on several album jackets from the 1970s and 1980s. I guess that was the decade she decided to give her name a foreign twist. *Pattai*. Is that Spanish? French? Italian? I'm not exactly sure. It really doesn't matter.

Mama Stories

I love her name.

And I love it because it belongs to my mother.

When my mother says my own name, she says it with much more flair than I ever have, or even wanted to. I remember once, when she accompanied me to a doctor's appointment during my teen years, she corrected me on its pronunciation.

"Your name", inquired the clerk, looking at her computer screen, fingers perched on the keyboard.

"Brittan," I said.

"Brittaaaan," corrected my mom.

I looked at her, and in my annoyed teenaged way, pronounced it the way I had for as long as I could say my own name to anyone who cared.

"It's Brittan. Brittan Swanagan."

Most of the time when I visit her at her assisted living senior living community, she reminisces about the Good Old Days. The stories play on repeat in her aging mind. Her eyes beam with unashamed pride when she reminds me that the Regal Theatre was once Bronzeville's pride and joy. The same legends that have slowly slipped away from this world were born into fame after local Chicago performances. Little Stevie Wonder. Marvin Gaye. Sam Cooke. James Brown. The Supremes. Those memories inevitably lead to more memories of her high school singing group, three girls and a guy skipping classes at Dusable High School, harmonizing to the radio they'd snuck in their backpacks. That's when she hits that note, that beautiful soprano note. It starts with her eyes closing gently and her fingers snapping in the air to the beat she hears in her head. And her heart. She leans closer to me, opening her eyes for a quick moment to emphasize what I already know.

"I could sing, girl. I *know* I could sing."

I know what comes next, so I try to keep her in those magical moments from past years, before she remembers that the guy in her high school singing group was murdered. More than likely because he was Black. And gay. Before she remembers that her coveted autograph book from those days was stolen. More than likely by her own blood relative. Before she remembers that her high school sweetheart died from a drug overdose. More than likely forever changing the course of her own vision of love. I'm usually left watching her tortured face as these thoughts begin to take detailed shape. I believe most people fight off their own demons, sometimes with success. But sometimes the efforts fail and we are back in that painful moment, whatever that may be. So, I change the subject, updating her on the grownish lives of her granddaughters, my daughters. Her face lights up again and she is back in the present moment, shaking loose the grip of her own haunting memories.

This mama story, my mama story, is a puzzle with a myriad of disconnected pieces. Fragments of events, situations, people, and places loosely scattered in my mind. I've always envied anyone who can chronologically recall childhood experiences with eerie precision. My friends are all able to effortlessly do this. It used to pain me, smothering me with intense pangs of loneliness and exclusion. Sometimes, I still feel this way, but mostly I sit in awe. It fascinates me and I've come to allow myself the privilege of sinking into their memories, although the ownership is not my own.

There are people who remember preschool. First grade. Second grade. Teachers. Friends. Clothes they wore. Addresses of former homes. Neighbors. Favorite pajamas. Friends' favorite pajamas. The favorite car of their favorite uncle. The scent of their eccentric aunt. Or the fragrance of their dad's cologne. Or their dad.

Three of my colleagues are this way, equipped with sharp memories. Crisp. I remember once, not too long ago, we were celebrating the end of what could probably be coined the worst school year ever. Tortilla chips, salsa, top-shelf margaritas, and taco platters had helped to clear everyone's head space, at least for a while. The conversation had moved from "kids these days" to "when we were kids", and I was sinking into the stories being told, eyes wide, head tilted to the right, and margarita in hand. The salty sweetness had loosened my lips.

"Y'all remember when we were in high school?" That was one of my friends.

"Yeah, girl!" That was the rest of them.

"Really?" That was me.

The conversation continued with me leaning more into their personal recollections, not particularly wishing that they were my own, but amazed at the fullness in which their memories took shape. The details of my teen life are fuzzy, at best. Somewhere, in the hallways of three different high schools in three different states, hides the sweetness of my first kiss, the sharpness of my favorite English teacher, and the excitement of getting my driver's permit. Unfortunately, my own mind constantly betrays me, giving me snapshots, but never full scenes. This sometimes leaves me bitter, confused, and mostly scared.

By the second round of drinks, the conversation grew louder. Scattered voices fought for attention, salsa beats pouring through the restaurant's overhead speakers. They were all laughing as they shared their memories, tipsy eyes filled with nostalgia.

I took another sip of my second margarita, sank a little further in my chair, tilted my head a little further to the right, and found a sliver of focus in my eyes.

"How the fuck do ya'll remember all that shit?"

The funny thing about memories is that they usually evoke one of two feelings: Happiness or sadness. For most of my life, I have tried to shy away from distorted memories of my childhood. I don't trust their accuracy. Ironically, most of them capture my mom's life and my life, intertwined, just me and her. My mother grew up without her father, without grandparents, without siblings. She did, unlike me, travel through her childhood and young adulthood with a host of beloved uncles and aunts. She was raised by her mother, who died two years before I was born. Here's where it makes sense. Here's the part that explains why I have, in many ways, tried to weave a life different from the one I experienced as a child.

Mama Stories

When I entered the world, my grandmother was gone. My father was never in the picture, having "gotten the hell out of Chicago" a month after I was born. Those are his words, not mine. California was calling him, an escape from everything (and everyone) in Chicago and the promise of the golden life he needed to create for himself. That left my twenty-five-year-old mother alone, with a newborn.

It also left me without grandparents on either parental side. Without siblings-I am my mother's only child and grew up not knowing my half-brothers. Without aunties or uncles-my mom is also an only child. Of course, there were scattered cousins a few states away and various people I loved because they loved me.

There were moves, many of them. There was confusion, lots of it. Different apartments in different cities with different schools. Most importantly, there was my mother, leading the way to a better life for me, for her. Somewhere on those interstate highways, new school hallways, and newest addresses, I stopped feeling grounded, connected. I know my mother cared for me with every ounce of her being, loving me with the essence of her soul, clinging to me as her everything. But, I moved into adulthood with some resentment. I often struggled to simultaneously find my feet and my breath, struggled to make sense of the jumbled mess of memories and my frequently changing realities. I've never stopped trying to find specific connections. Not just for me, but also for a mother who feels heartbroken when I can't recall more from my young life.

"Why can't you remember, Tanny? That's why I tried to give you good experiences as a child. Why don't you remember?"

"I don't know, Mom."

Around three years ago, during my very first appointment with my therapist, I sat on his couch and cried throughout my entire fifty-minute session. It wasn't until the third meeting that we were able to identify a starting place for my healing. He moved his yellow legal pad between the two of us and suggested I give a name to the swarm of bees that stung me each morning, leaving me doubled over in daily anxiety attacks.

My father.

My mother.

The inherited dark clouds from both.

"It's okay to be angry. You can feel anger and love simultaneously. It's not one or the other."

There was something cathartic about being given permission to own my feelings, this immense love in my heart towards the only person that has consistently been in my life from my very first breath. I now know that my love for my mother is not diminished by my regrets about my childhood, especially the parts that are lost somewhere in my adult mind. I can embrace anger as a real emotion without hating myself, without feeling that I have betrayed my mother in some way. More than anything, I can sink into the very clear memory that my mother always did the very best she could for me, mostly alone, and always with the one goal of protection. Even then, I knew that we were protecting and saving each other as we moved through life.

Mama Stories

I realize, through unabashed introspection, that much of who I am today is a direct result of my mother's choices for our lives. In turn, I'm learning to lean into these memories and make connections to my own life as a fifty-year-old African American woman raising two teen daughters into adulthood.

I guard several of my tangible childhood memories closely, such as my thirteenth birthday sleepover party. It was November 19, 1983, a chilled Saturday in Chicago. My mom and I were living in a rent-controlled apartment community on the far south side of the city, where most (if not all) of my favorite memories are the clearest, sharpest. We lived in a second-floor apartment from third through ninth grade. My mother had pushed all the furniture to the side of the walls in the living room so that we could have plenty of room for dancing, playing games, and eating picnic-style on the carpeted floor.

I remember the faces of my friends as they stepped into the entryway grinning ear to ear, excited for the evening's party plans. More than that, I remember my mama's beautiful cream-colored face opening into a bright smile, greeting each of them with wide arms, gently guiding them to the space designated for overnight bags.

I remember the excitement we held, waiting for our ice cream sundaes to be crafted to our individual, specific tastes. More than that, I remember my mama's eyes looking at each girl, making sure she felt included, satisfied. My friends were drawn to my mother. I remember being told I was lucky.

"Tell me if you want some more ice cream, baby. There's plenty."

I remember the album lyrics for Michael Jackson's *Thriller* taped to the wall while we recreated Michael's dance moves with uncoordinated, giggly tween bodies. But more than anything, I remember my mama dancing with us, adding harmony to Michael's soprano tunes, twisting and shaking her hips right along with us. I remember our eyes locking periodically throughout the night, and I remember feeling more love than I could ever hold in my heart…until I had my own daughters.

Perspective is everything. I am guilty, at times, of looking at my mother's choices for me through smudged lenses. I am ashamed of this, to this day. Although distorted, ragged memories haunt me occasionally, I know that I am in control of the narrative I share. I am in control of the narrative I lean into.

My mother is an amazing woman. I don't tell her this often enough, even though she sends me a text every Friday morning with the same message: "Happy Friday, my beautiful daughter."

My mother, the woman who managed to earn a college degree at the age of fifty, despite a string of starts and stops to focus on my needs.

My mother, the woman who raised me alone, without close family and without my father's presence, physically and financially.

My mother, constantly pushing through the darkness of her own pain and loss.

Mama Stories

My mother, the woman who never met a stranger, always looked into the hearts of others, and always tried her absolute very best despite mounds of obstacles, both internal and external in existence.

When I see her again, and she wants to revisit the days of sneaking backstage at the Regal Theatre, I won't try to stop her. She will talk about three girls and a guy, blending harmonies on the back stoop of her high school. She will close her eyes gently, left hand in the air to help her hit the high notes, walking cane in the right.

"I could sing, baby."

"You still can, Mama."

And I will take her hand and tell her what I should have been saying all along.

"Tell me again and again, mama, so that I can remember later."

Love Celebrated, Nurturing Remembered.

TOMI BANKS

Easter is a popular holiday, but I like to honor what it is to me—Resurrection Sunday. After all, there's so much more to it than Peter Rabbit, colored eggs, candy baskets and Easter outfits. In the time BC (before COVID), I'm sure you remember how we used to proudly don color coordinated suits, dresses, and patent leather shoes. I have fond memories of that time of year. It was an exciting time being a preacher's kid. The event run of show normally started two weeks prior to Easter weekend. Belk and Dillard's announced their Easter sales.

Layaway plans were commenced, grocery lists compiled, dinner meals planned and dessert recipes researched and debated. Shopping was a whole 'nother beast, but crazy fun. I felt like a star having my cousin Cheryl, Aunt Coco and Mommie argue over what I should wear and what my long, thick crown should look like when I recited my speech at the Easter pageant.

Mama Stories

Always the teacher, I can hear Aunt Coco giving me explicit instructions for my daddy, her brother, Reverend Thomas J. Banks, Jr. "Easter is Sunday and I must get your hair shampooed and pressed. Tell Tom to bring you down the hill in the morning so I can get started on your head. I want to get your Shirley Temple just right for Easter Sunday."

I can see Coco's brown styling stool so clearly. And I smell that beautiful atmosphere of smoke floating from the blend of Royal Crown hair grease and my thick hair under the heat from Coco's straightening comb. Hmmm, this was the process every Good Friday when my hair died by way of the Marcel heating stove, got rolled up on tissue paper and pink sponge rollers all day Saturday and then was resurrected Easter Sunday morning with springy Shirley Temples curls; the envy of many of my Sunday school friends.

Coco grew up in the 1940's in uptown Charlotte, North Carolina in a neighborhood called Brooklyn. 305 S. Davidson Street was the address for the Banks family. Located right in the center of the city, it was a Black neighborhood that was thriving with Black-owned businesses, churches, and homes. Coco was a cosmetologist by trade and even partnered in her own shop. I wasn't there back then. I came along when Coco, Grandma Gertrude, Sarah, and Daddy built a house at 314 Fannie Circle in the Grier Heights community. Our neighborhood was one of the many communities that was established after the Charlotte government 'reformed' Brooklyn for their own profit. Coco was the first entrepreneur I encountered. I watched her invite clients into her upstairs bedroom for a press and curl. Her clients bragged and praised her for being able to creatively croquignole and finger wave their hair with the most unusual common household item, a fork.

"Cora, you put a hurting on my head, and I know it's going to last for two weeks before I come back."

Cora was Coco's official name. I started calling her Coco as a child because I could not say "Aunt Cora". Coco could also rattle the pots and pans well--you know--cook! The entire Easter feast would be prepared by her.

She just happened to be employed by Mecklenburg County Schools. Coco was a cook at Billingsville Elementary School, the same school where Daddy had been a principal. Yes, I remember all the apple pies, icebox cakes, pound cakes, and sweet potato pies she baked. The pies were made with homemade crust. A mixture of Crisco lard, flour and a little salt and water. She used to let me help her roll the dough before she placed one round layer crust on the bottom of the pan and the second layer on top.

"You can take the fork and press the dough all around the whole pie, Thomasena. Make it pretty."

Helping with pies and rolling the greens was my responsibility when cooking with Coco. "Finish eating your grilled cheese and drink your apple juice. Then we will practice reciting your speech for Sunday. Now, did you memorize the second part like I told you? It's not hard, you just need to keep going over it."

Coco made sure I did my homework and knew my speeches. She truly worked hard to get me to count, multiply, and add in my head, but sometimes it just didn't take.

Mama Stories

"Thomasena, THINK, concentrate, it's just numbers!"

I wished to this day I could do arithmetic like her. Umph! But back to church business. Coco LOVED church! She got up in the mornings, at lunch and dinner, and went to bed talking about church. Even at 96 years of age, dancing daily with Alzheimer's and dementia, I could start a hymn and she would immediately chime right in, singing, whether she remembered the words or not. She had been a lifetime member of Clinton Chapel A.M.E. Zion Church singing in the choir, teaching Sunday school, and being a member of numerous church auxiliaries. But she reveled in the fact that her grandmother, Rachael Mosley, was a founding member of Clinton. Rachael had helped start Clinton under a grape arbor way back in 1810 with eight other founding members. In undergrad, this historical family event got me an A+ in my English Literature class. The professor begged me to publish it. Of course, I was equally ecstatic with j-u-s-t the A+ grade.

While Coco mastered the Easter feast, Mommie coordinated the Easter outfits. She made sure the latest and most fashionable Easter bonnets, matching dresses and jackets, laced ankle socks and polished patent leather shoes were always on deck. Growing up, fashion was one of the sure-fire ways Mommie and I connected. Walking in the door after school, I always loved to hear her say, "Thomasena, go check your bed. I got you something." Man, I flew to my room because that meant I had new clothes and shoes!

The most fabulous 'hugs' came when Mommie arrived back from her vacations in California. She would fly home bringing with her the coolest, weirdest outfits I ever could imagine. Mommie was eclectic, likely developed over the sixteen years she was stationed in what is believed to be the former Fort Parks Airforce Base in Dublin, California. She went into the Airforce as a registered nurse after receiving her degree from Kate Bitting Reynolds Memorial Hospital in Winston Salem, North Carolina. All those years in California groomed her to have an affinity for seafood, which we ate every Friday, along with sourdough bread and quiche: West Coast style.

I believe all those years serving as an officer meant Mommie shared fewer cuddly hugs with me than the ones I often envisioned mothers sharing with their kids. So, I learned to accept the beautiful clothes and brownies warm from the oven as my hugs. Hey, it just dawned on me while writing this story, this must be why I am in love with brownies! They remind me of her beautiful smile, strong soprano voice, muscular shoulders, dry joke telling, and weird ways of doing things. I never could figure out why she thought nailing artwork on the den ceiling was so cool. My sister and I never questioned her about it, we just shrugged our shoulders and laughed in our sister huddles.

Mommie was the epitome of a strong Black woman. All she had to do was look at you and that was it! One summer, I remember my arms and legs were adorned for two days with perfectly shaped butterfly welts. Mommie thought I had sucked my teeth at her, and I got spanked with the yellow butterfly fly swatter. Talking back and asking questions were not allowed. NEVER. Mommie held the rank of captain in the United States Airforce and after discharge, she married and became a RN at Good Samaritan Hospital in Charlotte (Good Sam). Good Sam was located where the Panthers' Stadium stands today and was the only African American hospital in the country during that time. Mommie's staunch military skills followed her into her role at Good Sam as a no-nonsense supervisor to newly employed nurses. My mom and her sister, Mrs. Hazel L. Byrd, quickly developed the reputation for unrefuted excellence on the hospital floors they supervised and were dubbed "The Stacks Sisters." I was amazed to hear the stories from nurses who had worked under my mom and auntie after I graduated and initiated my career in the medical field as a speech language pathologist. I am so grateful today for the high standards, life lessons, respect, survival skills and gratitude my mother taught me. Those attributes have empowered and blessed me to be the eclectic, creative adult woman I am today.

Those two women, not only raised their children, were entrepreneurs, military officers and held notable positions in their church and communities, but they were sisters-in-law and friends. They were known to plan fabulous dinner parties, entertain elders and bishops in their homes as well as tag team my dad to get what they wanted. They both held water (kept secrets) for years. I better not share those details in this book for decency's sake. But I do want to celebrate my mother, Daisy and Cora for the wonderful goals and accomplishments they achieved. Even in 2021, Mommie shows up on the news for her role at Good Sam and Coco holds a record for the work she did at Clinton Chapel. It amazes me that their contributions are still relevant and remembered today.

I will always remember their strength and excitement in this season. On a recent Resurrection Sunday morning, I was blessed with a 5:45 a.m. awakening. There will be no Easter lily outfit or huge Easter feast being prepared. I settled for being presentable for the Easter service on Zoom. I'm so grateful for resurrection memories, faith for a prosperous future, and two mamas who gave me their best

Love Celebrated. Nurturing Remembered

in their own unique ways. Who I am today is truly because of the nurturing, training, and love that Mommie and Coco instilled in me.

Love Celebrated, Nurturing Remembered...ALWAYS!

Mama Was Sanctuary
RITA SAMUELS

Mama prayed

She was brave and afraid. With seriousness and concern she taught us that, *kids don't know danger, but adults do.* Living in the rural, segregated South had taught her that truth.

It was Mama's home, the only one she had ever known. It was the place where the White Pond whispered words of life and the Pee Dee River's flood waters threatened to steal it away just as they had stolen the life of Mama's brother, Raymond, when he was only fifteen. It was the place where the KKK came to her brother Otto's house demanding to see his pretty, long-legged girls and the place where everyone on the other side of the trestle was family looking after one another--a sanctuary engulfed by uncertain times, racism, and poverty, but filled with richness in faith, love, and loyalty.

My mother gave birth to me on a cold, starry night in January when she was thirty years old. The dark dirt roads were without streetlights, making it pitch-black outside once the sun set on the Wash James estate where she, too, was born. There were no home phones for calling, so with a heavy silver flashlight in hand, my sisters,

Mama Stories

Martha and Squeaky hurried nervously through the path that led to the still, colorless house of Miss Rox and Miss Evalina. The light of the moon cast spooky shadows about them.

Although they were afraid to awaken the elderly women who had reprimanding tongues and icy looks for any child that crossed their paths or dared to enter their yard, the two siblings mustered up the nerve to do as they were told. Mama was in labor. She needed a midwife, and Miss Rox was the midwife who had delivered my sisters and most of my cousins. Although the civil rights movement was strong and making progress, Mama and my grandmother worried that the hospital, which was ten miles away, might not admit her to a delivery room without a long wait, or she might have to wait until after all the white patients had received care.

As she waited for Miss Rox, Mama could not help but remember the birth of Geraldine, her big, beautiful baby girl who passed away in the arms of my aunt Ruby soon after she was born, breaking the hearts of the whole family. That deep sadness, which would later be identified as postpartum depression, haunted her through the years but never conquered her strong will to experience a good life.

Miss Rox hurried through the briars to the old, humble house with holes in the roof and guided Mama to push me into the world where the stars of Aquarius peeped in to greet me as Mama whispered a prayer for me.

Mama provided

She was independent and vulnerable. Not long after I was born, Mama moved out of Grandma's house and into her own, without our father or any other man to depend on. She moved just a dirt road away to independence and finding herself. No doubt there were moments of vulnerability and uncertainty that accompanied the move, but not enough to change her mind. She worked and made do with what she had, and it was important to her that we learned, *things you can do for yourself - do*. Mama said not to *put faith in man, but trust in God*. And so, she did. Although the location was less than a half mile away from her mother's door, moving out to maintain her own residence was momentous. Like a songbird who had been fed and cared for, was Mama ready to fly on her own?

The echoes of loud hammering finally ended, and we moved into our small white wooden house on the hill. Inside, there was a shiny black living room suite, a round, fingerprint free glass table, new beds with comfortable mattresses, beautiful bedspreads, and pretty curtains for each room. The pecan-colored paneled walls radiated warmth, and in the living room was a picture of Jesus, standing at a door.

For entertainment, Mama had purchased a 13-inch color TV. My uncle Otto loved it best and stopped by every day of the first week to marvel at it when he completed his shift from his job at La-Z-Boy. But Mama's favorite was the stereo that had an AM/FM radio, 8-track tape player, and record player. It was my favorite, too. Late evenings when my older cousins got off from work, they would stop by for a hot plate and to hear, <u>I Stand Accused</u> by Isaac Hayes, or The O'Jays <u>Hooks in Me</u> which usually led to slow dancing couples and a lot of relationship talk that got us in trouble for listening to *grown folks' business*. It was hard not to hear grownups talking because the house didn't have much insulation. So that we didn't have to leave home to use the phone, Mama had one installed.

Mama Stories

The phone was attached to the wall in the kitchen, which was in the center of the house, making everyone vulnerable to eavesdroppers. You were simply going to hear someone else's phone conversation without trying or even wanting to. Therefore, people preferred to visit and chat if there was juicy gossip to spill rather than risk being overheard on the party line.

It was rare to have a phone and many of my relatives did not, so they would come to use Mama's. It seemed that we rarely used the phone because Mama was usually expecting a call and did not want the line to be busy. She enjoyed countless hours talking to her cousins and friends in Marion and Florence who were local and didn't cost long-distance fees. When Edward E. asked at school why my line was always busy, I was too embarrassed to respond.

Having her own place gave Mama the liberty to live as she decided each day. She stayed up late when she wanted and slept in when she could. At Grandma's house, only gospel music and hymns were allowed; dance music was considered sinful. But in her own home, Mama welcomed all genres of music, considering songs as medicinal as the teas she brewed to keep us healthy. In our new home, Mama taught us to work together and to take care of the things she worked so hard to provide for us. If we complained, she pulled out another life lesson to live by. In a soft voice she would say, *it's easier to do it right the first time than to have to keep doing it until you get it right.*

We took turns doing the dishes, hanging clothes on the clothesline to dry, folding the laundry neatly, and making beds properly. On Saturday mornings, we burned trash outdoors, mopped floors, dusted sand-filled rugs, and cleaned windows. We took turns pumping water for drinking, cooking, and bathing from the iron pump whose handle was difficult to bring down. Mama was a master at sneaking in life lessons. We learned that independence required hard work and that relying on yourself was liberating for young girls who often saw insecurities blinking back at them when they looked in the mirror. Those were all things we could do ourselves, so we did, and Mama created a secure place of calm in an unsafe world of violent protests and lynchings where Black women, children, and men felt vulnerable.

Uncertain times did not deter her. Mama continued making provisions for her family. The one I treasured most was the life-changing gift of indoor plumbing. We gladly loaded the carefully sorted laundry into our new washing machine and soaked in our full-length bathtub until our skin looked like golden raisins and the whole room smelled like Tone soap and Prell. In that tub, Mama soaked in her secrets and washed away her sins of the day.

Mama had some heroes who helped to shape her Black is beautiful teachings and soul restoration practices. She tackled the challenges of being a single parent like Fannie Lou Hamer wrestled for voting rights and better economic opportunities. Mama grew emboldened by the accomplishments of Shirley Chisholm who dared to be Black and proud enough to run for President of the United States. As Mama flipped through the pages of Ebony, Essence, and Jet magazines, she was empowered beyond her vulnerability. Her early steps toward self-reliance were nurtured through the articles she bookmarked and the pictures she saved. Those publications coupled with the scriptures from the Holy Bible Mama sometimes placed underneath her pillow gave her fortitude in unprotected spaces. She made a way—sometimes out of no way. Mama provided for us.

Mama shared

She was caring and fun. Our single parent home welcomed family and friends on weekdays and weekends where Mama shared life lessons, delicious homemade meals, and the latest music. Her yard parties were the best, bringing people who loved the Samuels family together from neighboring towns. When people came to Mama's house they stayed for hours because she made everyone feel like family. Mama wanted us to know that everybody is somebody, and not to joke about how someone looked, spoke, dressed, or smelled. She genuinely cared about others.

Byonnie came with his speech impediment, JC came with breath that begged for a mint, CC came in need of hair and body wash, and Boggs needed a dose of degreaser. But Mama listened to their stories and shared current events, the latest slang phrases, and petty gossip with them all. Monopoly, card games, and Pokeno consumed hours of fun times at the kitchen table. Mama cooked meals that stretched to feed the multitudes just like Jesus did with the two fish and five loaves. Somehow, there was always enough to eat and plenty of fun no matter how many cousins, aunts, uncles, and friends piled in.

Mama always said, the more, the merrier when asked how she liked having so many visitors in and out of her home. Once, DJ Davey brought his music system and everyone danced up a dust storm in our sandy yard doing the Bump and the Robot to <u>Dancing Machine</u> and going down the Soul Train line. To close out the fun we did the Hustle and the Bus Stop until the moths and lightning bugs from nearby fields joined in. We really did dance the night away. Mama shared what little she had with family and friends and made fun times, too.

Mama lived

She was adventurous and wary. Mama dared to do things that were not the norm in her family. Out of 15 children that her mother had, Mama, who was the baby of the family, was the only one to finish high school. She often told us of how shy she was to answer questions in class and that she wished she had better clothes to wear to the all-Black school she attended. Although Mama was wary and school was a challenge for her, she latched on to her new world of learning and succeeded. Mama wanted us to do better than she did.

Despite exercising caution, she became pregnant and did not go to college. The option for young ladies to take the pill wasn't available until 1952, two years after she had begun regularly sneaking down to Lover's Lane with James, the love of her life. Her life shifted to the responsibilities of parenting. Still, she instilled in us that we could be anything we wanted to be if we put our minds to it.

Like any mother, Mama wanted to see us achieve more and better out of life. When I graduated from Winthrop College, Mama and Aunt Ruby proudly made their way to my December commencement to see me become the first college graduate in the family. She displayed my degree on the mantle right next to her diploma and the diplomas of my sisters - a visual family legacy of intellect and perseverance. Later, Stacy the baby of our family, and I would each add a doctorate and a master's degree to the display.

Mama Stories

Throughout the years, she continued to warn anyone who listened, you'll never forget your first love. And she never did. Mama was gorgeous and had many suitors, but she loved James forever. When he married, she developed a complicated love with Rubin, who adored her, but feared marrying her would result in him losing his property, including the home he had bought his mother with money earned in the Air Force during the Korean War. They continued to love one another till death did they part. Love took them on long drives, where they listened to their favorite songs, visited the juke joints where they sat for hours laughing, talking, and dreaming of what could be, but never was. Mama had a traveler's heart. When my youngest sister, Stacy, was old enough, they traveled to other states on tour buses and explored new places with family and friends. They visited historical sites that had made national news and the pages of magazines as well as the locales we read about in those World Book encyclopedias she bought on an installment plan. When they visited the Lorraine Motel, where Martin Luther King Jr. was killed, she was a statue of somberness, taken back in time to her 40-year-old self. At dinner that evening, Mama whispered, *Keep trying to get to the mountain top*, while they dined on Tennessee sweet tea and barbeque ribs. Each trip was a history lesson wrapped in colloquial conversations with locals over delicious, unique foods that defined each city.

Along with traveling, Mama filled her young adult weekends with dance. She was a wonderful dancer. She ventured to surrounding towns in search of clean fun times of simply boogieing down to the sounds of her favorite songs. Mama came of age during a time when seat belts were not required, thumbing a ride wasn't given a second thought, alcohol was advertised in magazines, and no one knew the dangers of nicotine, so her generation came to love Pabst Blue-Ribbon, True-Blue cigarettes, and '65 Chevys. Mama lived with passion. She loved the excitement of doing things that were new and different. Mama gave herself permission to accept and enjoy her younger years. She actively participated in her life's journey every day. Mama lived.

Mama impressed

Mama appreciated beauty and beautiful things. Once she ordered a black pants suit with a red rose on the right leg and on the bottom left corner of the jacket. She loved that pants suit so much; she wore it when she was going to get down at the Cobra Club to Funky Town and to celebrate my sister's awards days at school.

She had beautiful, long hair, but would rock a sporty wig with a big city cut that made her look like a super model. Mama made Avon jewelry look like crown jewels and Sweet Honesty perfume smell like a million bucks. She made sure that we knew our Black was beautiful, covering the coffee table with African American magazines and photo albums of our family. We learned to be neat, clean, and confident by watching her. Some things Mama thought were beautiful were not so beautiful to my childhood eyes, like the time she bought a silver tree for Christmas and I cried because it was the most hideous thing I had ever seen. To make up for it the following year, she bought a white one. I cried again. I admit she was on the cutting edge of fashion and decor which my country girl cut-offs and nature-loving mindset had a tough time accepting. She dazzled. She was fashionable and impressive.

Mama Stories

Mama believed

She was faithful and obscure. As a child, Mama faithfully attended the United Methodist Church where the preacher's sermon was certain to get a few more snores than amens. It was the family's sacred place, so each generation attended with the obedience of Abraham and the faithfulness of Ruth. Grandma required her children to go to church and afterward, be ready to serve dinner to the preacher at her home. Mama would try to make herself obscure while she carefully poured his ice-cold Kool-Aid into Grandma's tallest crystal glass. The preacher was treated like a royal guest, but the youngest kids were overjoyed to see him leave since the custom was that children ate last.

When Mama was older, she and my sister Stacy started going to the services at a new holiness church called Mount Beulah. The loud bass guitars, tambourines, and organs made people leap from their seats, run up and down the aisles, and do holy dances. One Sunday, Mama was worshiping and clapping timidly when her hands suddenly grabbed her hips and her eyes looked up toward the ceiling, while her feet lifted from the floor. She held onto the pew and continued to jump up and down. When she came through, she was saved and filled with the Holy Ghost. She eventually settled into a Baptist church where she served as an usher, wearing the whitest whites and looking angelic as she strolled to the front of the church to get the communion trays or the collection plate, depending on which Sunday it was.

Mama believed the word of God, and she wanted us to know that *Jesus died for our sins, and He forgives us when we go down the wrong paths.* When my cousin got out of jail she did not shun, judge, nor fear him. She instead let us all know that Jesus said, *he without sin, cast the first stone.* It was puzzling to some, but she believed *faith could move mountains.* From her early days of prayer cloths from Reverend Ike who proclaimed, *you can't lose with the stuff I use,* to Jim Whittington, the televangelist to whom she sent prayer requests for many years, Mama always found comfort in God's word. She had a faith that brought her through dark times that she concealed from the world and turned over to Jesus. Mama believed.

Mama loved

Mama was perfectly imperfect. She had a prancing heart, dancing mind, and singing soul. She was every genre of music depending on her mood (and maybe the day of the week). When the Williams Brothers sang, <u>Dr. Jesus Said He'd Make Everything Alright</u>, it calmed her worries and soothed her anxious, often depressed soul. Raising girls in the South on a limited income wasn't easy, but she made it seem so. She poured a lifetime of love into the people she met, making lifelong friends who called, dropped by unannounced, and sent letters, gifts, and cards to her consistently through the years.

Mama loved people. She loved having visitors she called *company* at the house. Sometimes she laughed loudly at her own slightly raunchy jokes, other times she listened intently to the troubled hearts and minds looking for someone who cared.

When Estell and Nordric broke up, Mama knew just how to cheer up Estell by jokingly saying, *Wow, you liked him, didn't you? He must be was your first.* Loud laughter erupted across the room, scaring tear drops away to hide in corners of her eyes for a while. Mama sorted through her albums. She had the perfect song for every imperfect occasion. That night, she cued Betty Wright's <u>Tonight Is the Night</u> and the two did an analysis of the song that humored them both and brought back the vibrance of life by being tickled to death with a conversation that shouted, <u>I care</u>.

Mama even disciplined with love. When we were sassy or not doing what we were told, Mama punished us and said, *I'm doing this because I love you. It hurts me more than it hurts you.* She would caution us too saying, *one day you gonna wish you weren't so grown. Better enjoy being a child while you can.* Oh, how right she was.

Parents never admit that they have a favorite child, but everyone knew Mama did. Although she denied it, Mama loved her first born best. When my oldest sister got pregnant on the same day she lost her virginity, Mama tried to have the perfect words to say, but she couldn't hide her worry. Squeaky had already announced her pregnancy a month prior. The news of becoming a grandmother was bittersweet and Mama took the news of the pregnancy like I took the unpalatable Father John's cough syrup. She seemed to daydream while holding on to the kitchen sink. Mama's rice was usually a pot of pure perfection, but that day, she scorched it. The house was unusually quiet and still for weeks. Mama loved her children and those beautiful grandbabies with all she had in her perfectly imperfect way. Mama loved us all.

Mama left

Just a few miles from the White Pond that whispered life and the place where her childhood house once stood, she laid her head down to sleep as Aquarius peeked in from its highest point in the night sky.

Mama left us that night to be with the Lord on October 17, 2017. Those frequent and infrequent visitors that she had known for a lifetime stopped by for a week to say farewell to the lady who had loved them indicating, indeed, they loved her back. The weeping willows in the front yard wept along with so many hurting hearts. There was no Peace Lily could comfort the sorrow in our souls.

Mama's own heart had broken in June when her beloved, a victim of heart-wrenching elder abuse, suffered and died. That kind of evil tormented her spirit because she believed in being good to others and causing no harm. If she hurt someone's feelings accidentally, she quickly apologized and said, *I didn't mean no harm.*

Mama left a legacy of lessons that we still follow and pass on to the next generation. She never claimed to be perfect and didn't *put on airs* either. Once in a blue moon, with the same girlish giggle of her youth, she might jokingly ask her guests for a sip of their beer, which she really didn't want, or for a cigarette, that she really did. When Mama found Jesus, she lost her taste for beer, but nicotine won most of the cigarette battles they had through the years. We learned to appreciate Ecclesiastes chapter 3 from her, including:

There is a time for everything,
and a season for every activity under heaven:
a time to be born and a time to die,
a time to tear down and a time to build,
a time to weep and a time to laugh,
a time to mourn and a time to dance,
a time to be silent and a time to speak,
a time to love and a time to hate,

Mama Stories

a time for war and a time for peace.

Mama's good outweighed all her bad. So, in the words of Shirley Caesar who she loved, we remember Mama in a happy way.

Cora Samuels, Mama, left us with a passion for life, a guide and vison for the future, and memories of the past. She left us with faith, grace, and love to sprinkle like seeds across the world.

Juanita's Gift
MONICA BROWN NASH

I remember the day I met my mother's father. The grandfather I grew up knowing and lovingly referred to as "grandaddy" was not my mother's biological father. He was the only grandfather I had ever known, and my mom had always called him Dad. He never made any distinction between sisters and the rest of his grandchildren when our parents loaded us all up on the train from Chicago to Alabama where we spent our summer visiting him and my grandmother. As children, we never felt any difference. My mother always referred to him as her father and the four of us always called him Granddaddy.

All that changed one lazy Sunday afternoon after our family moved from the south side of Chicago to Tuscaloosa, Alabama. We had only been in Tuscaloosa a few months when my mother came into the living room where the four of us were watching mindless television and announced that her father was in town and if anyone wanted to meet him to be ready in ten minutes. Now that we lived a short distance from where my mother grew up with the people we thought were both her biological parents, no one considered tagging along until my sister asked, "What's Grandaddy in town for?"

Mama Stories

My mother's response shook me. "Not your grandfather, *my* father," she said. My two oldest sisters didn't budge, but my sister Yolanda and I exchanged startled looks. Who was my mother talking about? Wasn't her father the granddaddy we knew and loved and visited every summer and taught us where milk "really" came from? Wasn't her father the one who would drive into the tall grassy fields as we swung our legs on the back of his pickup truck and laughed as the grass tickled them? Wasn't my grandfather the man who took us to the watermelon patch and burst sweet melons over the edge of the truck so we could eat the warm, juicy flesh?

My grandfather loved us and taught us about respecting the land they cultivated, never trying to get more than the earth could bear. My grandfather lived to help others. He and my grandmother believed in God, and it showed. They were always helping others who were less fortunate. People would come by the house after dark and my grandparents would go outside and talk to folks who needed help. I never knew who they were or where they came from, but my grandparents seemed to know them and their stories. Later I learned there were some people who only came around after dark so others wouldn't see them asking for help to feed their children. My grandparents never turned anyone away and everyone who came, came only because they needed help. Those who knew my grandparents would come up from the backwoods around their house, calling out before they got to their front porch so they wouldn't startle us. They knew their grandchildren were city folk and startled easily. The entire community was made up of farmers then, but those were the less fortunate folks who didn't have anything to barter with and no means to pay my grandparents back.

Juanita's Gift

My grandparents always gave to those less fortunate without making them feel bad about asking. That was how they lived.

Then, it hit me. My mother must have been speaking about her *birth* father, a family secret whispered amongst us, but never spoken to us. As the realization washed over me, I remembered that my mother was the oldest and she had a different last name than her siblings. We had never asked, and no explanation was ever given. When they began to discuss a subject that we weren't supposed to hear, a hush would come over their conversation and someone would give us a chore to do or tell us to go outside and play. We were never allowed to sit and listen to grown folks talk, and we knew better than to ask.

My sister and I dressed quickly, figuring that our mother wouldn't wait. As soon as we were ready, we ran to the living room just as our mom reached for the keys to the car, and my sister and I ran out the door behind her. My mother never enjoyed driving. She drove out of necessity and panicked behind the wheel, driving so fast that it was frightening. My sister and I jumped in the back seat immediately so our mother wouldn't be distracted as she drove to Mrs. Mays' house. We sensed she would need to focus during the short drive, so we remained silent. As I watched her speed through the streets, hands gripping the wheel of our family car, I wondered what she was thinking. Was she nervous about meeting her dad as a grown woman, married with children of her own? Her determination to put her fear of driving aside to see her father told me meeting him was important to her. My sister and I were curious to learn anything about our mom's father since we knew nothing about him. As we pulled up in front of Mrs. Mays' house, I saw the relief on my mom's face as she turned off the ignition.

Mrs. Mays was my grandmother's closest childhood friend since grade school. She was the one who called my mom that Sunday and told her that her father was in town. Mrs. Mays had moved from the small farming town in Tuscaloosa where she and my grandmother had grown up. Mrs. Mays married a man that could build anything. He had added a room to the back of their home with a side entrance where Mrs. Mays made a comfortable living doing hair.

Mrs. Mays welcomed us in and offered us refreshments. We immediately responded in unison, "No thank you." My sister and I were too nervous about meeting the mystery man. Mom entered Mrs. Mays' living room holding both of our hands. Maybe she was a bit anxious to see her father, a man she had apparently not seen for years. Mom hugged the man we had never met who stood up to greet her as a look of surprise filled his face. There was his daughter, flanked by two skinny little girls with long ponytails, and he seemed to be caught off guard by our presence.

Mom introduced us, "These are your two youngest grandchildren. The two oldest ones are attending the University of Alabama," she said proudly. The stranger stooped down to greet us at eye level, giving us a gentle hug and then shaking our hands delicately. All I knew about him was that my mom had his last name, and I had an opportunity to find out everything I could—not by asking questions, but by listening.

I didn't know it then, but I was meeting the person that held the unspoken truth of Mom's birth and my grandmother's shame. He was my mother's father, and just like any other well-kept family secret, his presence raised questions in me that I was sure would never be answered. I was too young to understand what had happened between them, which is why the encounter was so significant to me.

My sister and I sat across from Mom and her biological father, our thighs rubbing against the thick plastic that covered the cushions of Mrs. Mays' flowered couch. I tried to ignore the uncomfortable plastic, unphased by the sharp edges that scratched the back of my legs, as Mom and the one she called her father sat across from us in two chairs flanked by a small table.

I stared as Mom engaged in small talk as if the years had passed with them staying connected. Without hesitation, Mom gave him the respect that one might earn if he had been a part of her life all along, but one of my grandmother's confessions to me was that my mother's father had only had a few encounters with her when she was in grade school.

Their encounter that day was laced with pleasant tones, dignity, and respect. He seemed proud to be meeting his daughter, a grown woman with well-behaved children—his grandchildren. I was surprised that my mother didn't treat him like the stranger I thought he was to her. She spoke to him with ease, having no malice or hurt in her words. They spoke slightly above a whisper and I hardly heard their exchanges about life and family because I was too busy drinking him in.

He was wearing a brown suit with shoes and socks that matched. My grandmother was an excellent seamstress, and even though I didn't know at the time what tailor-made meant, I could tell that the suit he wore was expensive and had been made just for him. He was very articulate with dark smooth skin and a kind, round face, and he had my mom's smile. He laughed heartily about something he and my mother shared, and he carried himself like someone who had not been pulled down by the segregation and discrimination of the South where he and my grandmother spent their childhood. His hands were beautifully manicured and didn't appear as if they had ever seen a hard day's work. It was obvious that Mom's dad was a man that made his living away from the fields.

He was personable and engaging, just like Mom. My sister and I remained silent while the itchy plastic cover forced me to readjust my position. I barely breathed as I watched the two of them get reacquainted, talking to one another in familiar tones.

I listened as Mom spoke about us with pride as she periodically glanced at my sister and me who were sitting like statues watching their every move. She interjected bits and pieces about our lives in the conversation with her father (as if he could get to know us in one visit), and he would periodically look over at us as he and Mom talked about things that they were comfortable discussing. With two sets of eyes watching, as though they had kept in touch over the years, we stared and tried to pretend we weren't listening as we sat quietly observing the man who wasn't "granddaddy," but was a man Mom referred to as her father.

I stared as they talked casually about things that didn't matter to me. I knew better than to interrupt their conversation with questions my twelve-year-old self wanted to ask, but I hoped that their conversation would unlock the mystery of what happened years ago. I was hoping to learn the origin of my mom's "secret dad," which no one was willing to tell us anything about, but the conversation about the past never came up. Whatever happened in the past so many years ago would remain a secret because, for them, it was settled.

I didn't know how I felt about him. I couldn't put what I was watching into words that made sense. Their conversation was all about the present—how Mom, her husband, and her children were all doing. They seemed only interested in moving forward. Mom's father, a stranger to me, was beaming with pride at his daughter and the two youngest grandchildren he had just met, but all I could think about were questions I wanted to ask that would have made us all uncomfortable.

What happened? Why was he such a secret all these years? Does he have a family—grown children and grandchildren? Does his wife know about Mom?

Even if I had conjured up the nerve to ask, my mother would have cut me to the quick. She would view my questions as rude and an invasion of her privacy. I could tell that my mother was happy to spend time with her father and when their conversation ended, my mom gave her dad a warm hug. I stared as they embraced, Mom's eyes slightly watering and her dad smiling and holding her by her shoulders, seeming to take her entire being in.

As Mrs. Mays came out from the back room of her house, he walked us to our car, wrapping his arm around Mom's shoulder. He briefly hugged me, then my sister and we jumped in the back seat of the car while he and Mom continued their goodbyes. The drive home was as quiet as the drive up. I didn't feel comfortable asking my mother what she was thinking or how she felt about the time she spent with her dad. We were raised not to ask questions like that, but I still wondered.

Years later, while attending the University of Georgia, I took a Greyhound bus from Georgia to Alabama to spend my Thanksgiving break with my grandparents. They were much older and were slowing down. It was the first time I had ever visited them without being accompanied by members of our family. The house seemed eerily quiet with just my grandparents and me. The three of us ate a delicious Thanksgiving meal with all the trimmings. There were always delicious made-from-scratch desserts at my grandparent's home, and my grandmother had made my favorite—sweet potato pie! I understood why they wanted all the grandkids to visit each summer, filling the house with laughter and giggles.

I gathered up the courage to ask my grandmother about Mom's father that Thanksgiving weekend. I figured that any wounds or regrets she may have held onto over the years were long gone.

My grandmother told me their story, how they got together, and why they never married. His people lived too far away and her father, my great-grandfather, didn't want my grandmother to be surrounded by folks she didn't know without having her own family members nearby. My great-grandfather refused to give my grandmother his blessing and my grandmother wouldn't leave home without it. She loved her father and didn't want to disappoint him any more than she already had. I sat at the small kitchen table cramped with the Thanksgiving meal we had just eaten. My grandmother began gathering up the leftovers and putting them away. She walked to her kitchen window, her back turned to me. I remained silent as she washed the same dish continuously. Was she thinking about our conversation, about the love she lost? Was she wondering what her life might have been like if she had made a different choice? Whatever she was thinking, she kept it to herself. I didn't try to make conversation with her, it wasn't my place to interrupt her thoughts, but I'm sure my questions had awakened her memories.

The house remained quiet and began to fill with heaviness. It was as if I could feel the memories of her past hovering in the room, but only for a moment. I remained silent, not wanting to ask anything further. She had shared what she wanted me to know, and I was okay with that.

It never occurred to me to ask my grandmother if my mom's name held a specific meaning or what her thought process was when she named her. While writing this piece, I looked up my mother's name for the very first time. I will never know for sure, but I believe my grandmother deliberately named my mother Doris. A name that means "a gift."

My Girl

TIFFANY GRANTHAM

I've been beaten down by society's belief that a husband and children are a necessity once you turn twenty-five. Holidays are the worst and often include rapid-fire questions from well-meaning family members such as, "When are you getting married? You do want children, right? Don't you like men?" Then they complain when I show up to the holiday dinner late and jet before they can finish folding the aluminum foil over my plate. Yes, I'm dodging their questions. They don't realize how close I am to a violent reaction.

Being single and childless is a shadow that follows me wherever I go, even on my brightest days. What brings me down even more are the questions that come from other women. I'd think they would understand. Instead, they gang up on me too, as if a woman's main goal in life should be to get married and start popping out babies as soon as possible. Society, family and friends haven't been the only ones beating me down about marriage and kids. I've felt the pressure internally, too.

Mama Stories

I'm getting closer to forty as I countdown to my thirty-fourth birthday. I'm debating how to make this birthday as special as some of the others I've celebrated. Last year was small and intimate with the theme of "For The Love of Tiffany." You guessed it; the party was all about finding me a date. I've spent my last three birthdays as a single woman and had bad luck reeling in a serious boyfriend, it was time to take action.

Dating has given me more lessons than love. I've often felt like I was last in the line for blessings when everyone close to me received what I've been waiting for. I spent many days wondering what I was doing wrong, crying because even when I thought I was doing the right thing it never seemed to work out in my favor. I felt betrayed for not getting what I thought was owed to me. After terrible breakups, dodging others, and working on myself in the process, I thought surely my time would come.

My Girl, as I like to call my mom sometimes, was my anchor during those times. One time, I cried to her about my soon-to-be ex-boyfriend, afraid of being alone—single forever. The movies never show you it's okay to be alone; at least none that I'd ever seen. Being single in the movies was equal to misery. A relationship meant happiness. I told her of our plans to move in together and how much it upset me that our relationship was falling apart.

When I tell My Girl something about the people in my life, she never forgets. She's my first and forever ride-or-die best friend. My mother's the type to gently remind me of the things I told her. With patience that surely mimicked Job's, she listened to my snotty-nosed crying over the phone, barely able to catch my breath.

"Do you remember what he did when you were on a phone plan together?"

I did. That was the first time I called her upset over something he did.

"And I'm sure there are other things he's done you haven't told me about,

but I'll let you have those." she continued; and she was right.

"Think about it baby, you were already paying both halves of the phone bill. What do you think he would've done if you were to move in?" I was quiet.

She was right, again. The bills would've been paid mostly by me no matter whose name was on them. We sat on the phone in silence. I kept whimpering, trying to let common sense wash over me. It was hard. I thought and felt like my world was crumbling around me. I was twenty-five with a failed relationship, working two part-time jobs and not a clue what I wanted to do next with my life. My Girl let me sit on the phone and cry without judgment or interruption. That's what a loving hug feels like. Since she lived in Orlando and not a few hours away like before, the virtual hug would have to do.

"I want you to live on your own so you know how to take care of yourself and know what it's like," Mom said breaking the silence. "Travel, just really enjoy life before you decide to start a life with someone."

Over my sobbing, I heard her, but it would take a while for the words to sink in.

Now that I'm firmly in my thirties, I finally understood what she was trying to tell me. Her desires for my life were not unreasonable or selfish. She gave advice that came with freedom I couldn't understand until now. I began living out my mother's request with gratitude. There were days I would sit on the couch and look around my apartment and think, *this is what she meant.* Life up to that point was going great. I was in school, dating, traveling—enjoying life.

Christmas of 2018, my brothers and I flew to Florida like we do every year. It was the one time of year I looked forward to my mother's cooking and spending time with family. After a game of spades, my mother told my brothers and me she had recently been diagnosed with stage three lung cancer.

"They found a tumor," I remember hearing before her voice started to hollow out, sounding further and further away. For the next six months, I was on edge—always on the verge of tears or crying at work, at school, on the phone with friends; in the shower, and even in the grocery store. Work-related issues gave way to attention from HR, making matters worse.

One night while at a friend's house, we watched a reality show on TV. On the show, someone's husband received news that his father died from lung cancer. The coincidence was unexpected and so were my tears. It felt as though I had been holding everything in since my mother told me the news.

Life became tentative. Every corner felt like something lurking, waiting for me to change my life forever. In addition, my biological clock began ticking louder than ever from the time I awakened in the morning until I closed my eyes at night. Everything reminded me of my parents' age, their declining health, and my childless state. The world had somehow crawled onto my shoulders to rest. I spent my days wondering if I would ever have children; and if I did, with who? Would my parents be young enough to truly enjoy them? Would my children be old enough to remember their grandparents?

On my drive back home, I reflected on some of our best times--me flat twisting and picking her salt and pepper afro, watching her slide on her croc sandals and saying, "They're so comfy," as if she was telling me for the first time and not the fiftieth. I remembered those times of holding her hand adorned in silver and white gold rings and hearing the clanking of her bracelets. I wanted to hear her light and giggly laugh forever, or hear her say "Hey my baby girl," in a way that only she could. I wasn't ready for any of those memories to be the last, so I spent the next few weeks thinking of ways to remedy the situation and our time together.

I decided to take a class, but while sitting in class, my thoughts split between the lesson and how I was going to fix "my problem." I don't spend a lot of time worrying; I fix what I can and leave the rest to the universe. But this, this, I knew I could fix. The immediate solution was to ask a trusted friend who I had known since my freshman year in college. Over the years, I watched his growth as he learned who he was as a man and a father—present and dedicated. There was a sense of trust I had with him that I didn't have with anyone else. So, the plan was to ask him, then tell my mother I did at-home insemination--easy. After class, I mustered up enough courage to make the call.

"Hey," I said, gripping the steering wheel tighter. *'We're here now. No turning back.'*

Mama Stories

"I have a question to ask you." *It was now or never.*

"What's up?" he asked. I could hear the skepticism in his voice—he knew he could never really tell with me.

"What if I asked you to give me a baby?" A red light; the noise of traffic ceased and I held my breath waiting for his answer.

After what seemed like an eternity, he finally said, "But we're not even dating." I heard a bit of interest or at least curiosity in his voice as I'm sure he wondered *"Where is she going with this?"*

"That's not what I asked you. I would have the baby," I clarified.

I heard a brief sigh of understanding, then he finally responded.

"I don't want to raise another child that's not living with me, and I can't knowingly have a child with someone and not be there for them."

And just like that, my plan folded. A part of me knew it was a lot to ask, but I was willing to take the risk. As much as I respected his decision, his commitment to being responsible was keeping me from giving my mother the grandchild she didn't ask for. We hung up shortly after, my reasons not discussed.

A phone call to my mother was next— our second phone call of the day. During my drive to school and walk to class was our usual talk time, so when I called, she answered with the same excitement as always, "Hey girl, you lonesome on your ride home?"

I laughed, "No, I have a question to ask you." I take another deep breath and say, "Do you want any grandkids?"

"Are you dating? I didn't know you were dating?" she quickly asked.

"No. I'm not, but do you want them?"

She paused, "Well, how would I get them?"

"I would do at-home insemination," I said, revealing my great plan.

There was a brief sigh from her which I knew well. It's given with a slight tilt of her head to one side with a bit of sadness. I'd seen it over the years during our heartfelt conversations.

"No!" she exclaimed. "I want them to have a mommy *and* a daddy."

I said okay, then our love yous and goodbyes, and ended the call.

Deep down I was relieved I didn't have to change my life in an instant. No more thoughts of impending cost calculations of treatments and medications because it's not covered by insurance in my state.

I'm not sure what the conversation was between her and my middle brother. I can only imagine her asking him if he was offering her some grandchildren too because shortly after our conversation, I received a text from my him: "You giving out grandbabies?!"

Both plans ended as fast as they were conceived. The questions still loom and the tick-tocking is worrisome at times, but I can rest assured I'm accepted by my mother with or without a child. Because of her, I know my life is not defined by when and how many times I reproduce.

Mama Stories

My Girl helped me realize that time is, relatively, on my side in that there is no need to rush to live life. Things will happen when and how they should. My job is to live purposefully and trust in divine timing.

In the meantime, I've been granted a few more (and hopefully many more) years to be called Lil' Sheila by friends and family when I'm with My Girl; seeing my brown skin and her golden tan are our only differences. I've been granted more years to hear her laugh, retell stories from her past, talk about current news, and all the little joys in between.

I take a deep breath before my heart begins to race with anxiety at the thought of being single. "It's okay, the world didn't end." I let out a long sigh that turned into a chuckle. There are mornings where I'm completely grateful for being unattached--much like today.

The sun is still resting underneath the clouds as my coffee begins to brew. The only sound heard is the gurgle from the coffee maker. The birds are still asleep and I'd imagine the rest of the world is nestled cozily under covers. It's quiet; the type of quiet you'd feel ashamed of disturbing. Like being allowed to sit in a forbidden place if you are seen and not heard. I pour my coffee slowly clockwise over my milk to stir the two. The aroma of cinnamon and hazelnut carry me to my dining table.

Here, I have a perfect view of the sky. The sun peeks through turning cloudy skies to soft lavender and orange. The birds begin to sing their morning praises and I listen intently. They sing a song of gratitude I cannot express and only God can understand. Sun rays begin to creep through open blinds making my living room a perfect picture of tranquility.

Today, my place is clean. Everything is in its place, my plants watered, my books stacked perfectly, and the lines in my carpet make me feel accomplished. *Thank you,* I say softly before taking my first sip; remembering when having my own place was a distant dream and now sitting at a table I put together.

I'm thankful for the quiet that will one day be replaced with early morning requests from needy children such as, "Mommy can I?" or "Mommy can you?" or, "Honey, where's my...?" from a husband who can never remember where his things are. The desire for this life continues but is yet to be fulfilled. However, the desire to be whole, to learn who I am, what I'm capable of, and what I want takes precedence.

Life should be lived intentionally, fully present, and authentically with the ones we love most, not dictated by events on a false timeline. I'm so grateful for my mother and my experiences for helping me to have confidence in my current choices.

Pass The Mic

A Mother's Life Lessons Through Song

YAYA S.

Musical Muse: "Message in our Music" – O'Jays

Ma may have left us in body, but her spirit and lessons live on for generations.

Most days Ma could be found rushing home after work, picking up the kids from Moah's house, then rushing around the corner to our two-story townhome style apartment to get ready. It was a tradition: Fridays at Nawma's and LLoyd's. I remember my mother throwing house parties with family members and friends on Friday nights at our home. They played spades, bid whist (I could NEVER figure that one out), often drinking Miller High Life, their drink of choice. Then there was dancing, lots of dancing and there may have been some plant love *(we're talking trees, reefer, Mary Jane)*, 'cause it was 1973 and the funk movement was in full effect.

In my view, my mother led the funk ship. Beautiful eyes, shining like bright beads, full 'fro--or was it a wig? She was the queen of versatility, influencing me and my love of transformation through hair. Oh, and that smile. She could have lured the masses and birthed a NATION with the power of her attraction. She was so bad she was known to rock a golden crown; perhaps to let everyone know they were in the presence of a queen.

Call her Mama Badass. But then it all disappeared. Tiptoed out of the room like a thief afraid of getting caught. Was it grief that robbed us of her soul? Yes, death. Everything changed when she lost Moah, her grandmother. EVERYTHING.

Friday night parties were afros, bell bottoms, fancy cars, good music, great libations, loving family, and funkdafied friends, and it also meant I'd be allowed to dance for just a little bit. Any other night, y'all know damn well my mother wasn't gonna let me hang around grown folks' business. Any other night there'd be no discussion, I'd just have to act accordingly. That's who my mother was. She was a straight shooter, and some found it difficult to accept. She really didn't give a damn most times. I'm sure she originated IDGAF, way before acronyms and the digital world. On those nights I spoke, I ate, I danced, and I went in the room with my big sister, Suzie.

Now let's give my mother her proper introduction. We called her Ma. I don't know why, and I never asked, 'cause I learned real early that to effectively navigate my mother, I couldn't ask any questions. I learned what I needed to learn on a "need to know basis." I think that is why I am so curious to this day.

What's that? Why? When? How? Yeah, those questions would never have worked with Ma, not without experiencing some powerful stares and sarcastic responses. I learned to pick my battles. That's how I survived, and I made it out okay, I guess.

That night, forty-eight years ago, began my love for Ma's favorite music. The music provided a sense of hope, encouragement, understanding, and a few booty-shaking opportunities. Ma loved a variety of music, including Funkadelic. She was a sassy soul and she incorporated life lessons in some of her favorite songs. Those lessons covered topics such as individual freedom, committed relationships, from forgiveness to love and from regret to live life out loud.

Pass the mic is my story encouraging the conversation around trauma, grief and abandonment, but ultimately using the lessons from Ma's favorite songs to make it OUT and to break generational curses one funky song at a time.

Thee House Party

The wagon crisp white lettering was big enough for my sister and me, but she let me ride in it alone. She was five years older than me, so I looked up to her. In our townhome community, there was a hill in front of the home where we lived. On that hill was another set of townhomes, and their parking spaces were out front. My sister Suzie and I quickly walked up the hill as she pulled the wagon behind us. She was strong and on a mission. Once at the top of the hill, Suzie positioned the wagon so I could jump in and when I did, she turned the wagon around, I felt a big push, and the next thing I knew I was hurtling toward the bottom of the hill as the wind whooshed past my ears. I wasn't sure if I should have been excited or afraid.

As my four-year-old life flashed before my eyes, I couldn't stop thinking about Ma's Friday night party. Would I survive so I could attend? I remember hearing my mother's voice yell out, "Suzie!" But there was nothing I could do because the wagon hit something, maybe a large rock, and thus began my short acrobatic career. I twirled through the air and landed face down on a rock. I don't remember much after that, maybe I blacked out. I have a little souvenir from that day--a dent in my forehead.

I don't remember getting in trouble, or anybody being really concerned about my injury. I don't know why. Maybe because it was Friday night and we were all too busy preparing hearts and minds for the party. Even at four years old, I was excited. I could hear the chords from one of my favorite songs in my head. A song that made the walls jump, "Now I lay me down to sleep, Oooh, I just can't find a beat." But they always seemed to find the beat. "Flashlight" by Parliament was Ma's JAM...well one of them. She loved music. She'd get herself up and shake what my grandmama gave her.

My mother always reminded me of how special I was and how important I was to her. She let me know how proud of me she was, even when I wasn't so proud of myself. Sometimes we can be so hard on ourselves. She wanted me to be the best, be *with* the best and do the best. I fell short at times and that was oh so hard. What I know now is that she really wanted me to do my best, even when things aren't going so well. She encouraged me to never let anyone dim my light.

Song Lesson #1: Everybody's got a little light under the sun. Never let anyone dim your light, even when you may not feel your best.

Ma was a roadrunner and often we would end up clear across town because she was going wherever she wanted, whenever she wanted, however she wanted. Independent? Not so much. Determined? You betta believe it. She was driven, and a lil' bossy too. She stayed busy, over-committing, and aways stepping in where needed, but then something happened. Whatever IT was became a traumatic experience, an open sore left to fester and take forever to heal. Things changed. Depression must have set in and her zest for life faded. As a kid, I watched all of it unfold, but I didn't understand why it was happening. As an adult, I have a better understanding. Ma had been traumatized by Moah's death and was unable to cope. As a result, she traumatized her children, leaving us to either traumatize our loved ones, or get the help we needed to bring the cycle to a close. If only we had known then that grief could lead to trauma and the effects could impact generation after generation. Instead, we judged, accused, and isolated.

Miller Brewing Co.

One of Ma's favorite songs was "One Nation Under a Groove" by Funkadelic, created by the incomparable George Clinton. Listen, that's my song now, too. It reminds me so much of her daily drive when she worked at Miller Brewing company. Ma said she would turn on "One Nation Under a Groove" at the beginning of her commute and jam the ENTIRE time. The song would be coming to an end just as she pulled into the employee parking lot in her red Volkswagen bus. Yup, she was one cool mama. I believe in traditions, and you can best believe we will continue to "Dance our way out of our constrictions," as one line from that song proclaimed. The song begins with a few verses that talk about how hard things can be.

This is exactly how many of us feel when backed into a corner. We've felt stuck, isolated, unsupported, hurt, and hopeless, but like the song suggests, we must find a way to dance ourselves out of our constrictions and figure out how to break the chains of what's holding us back.

I remember when Ma lost Moah. I watched Ma's joy leave when Moah passed away. I can imagine Ma listening to that song, expressing how deep the pain of love and loss can be. She was in such a deep, lonely place during that time and long after. Wonder how I know? I experienced the same dark place after losing Ma. Because I experienced it, I decided to approach my loss differently, determined to make it out for me, my children, and our legacy.

Song Lesson #2: This is a chance. This is a chance, to dance your way out of YOUR constrictions. Sometimes WE'RE the ones holding ourselves back and we need to break free from our limiting beliefs.

Although Ma dealt with grief, pain and depression that seemed unbearable at times, she just kept dancing her way out of each situation whether it was from the constraints of mind or imagination. So, every time you see me dance and I am spinning, singing, smiling and full of joy, just know I am dancing with Ma and freeing myself from distracting patterns which will trap me into believing suffering is common and to be expected. Trauma is real, let's break free.

Live out Loud

Very rarely did I hear my mother speak of love in any shape or form. It was a bit strange. She never spoke of the "love of her life," or shared the love story of her and my father. I wonder if my mother ever really knew what love was. Now, what she DID speak clearly about and what she instilled in me today is, "Don't you EVER date an ignorant man." Well, okay den!

Ma had no problem expressing herself in other ways. She was the first to give zero fuchs in the 1980s before it was trendy. The more I think about it, Ma never really told me what to do. She made sure I knew what NOT to do. And the more I thought about it, the more I realized it was the exact place where I learned the distinct skill of identifying what is wrong and immediately creating a plan, often unsolicited. For the most part, it's a beneficial skill, but there are times when the feedback can blow up in your face.

Everybody talks about addiction, but nobody talks about the pain behind the addictive behaviors. Imagine having your loved ones constantly badger you to get help, to get better, to leave the situation, or simply stop. How does one stop the pain of losing someone when the fact remains that person will never return? It's not the addiction a person needs to heal from, it's the pain and loss that needs to be worked through. There's often guilt, regret and emptiness, and then surrender. I've found the person dealing with all the pain finds themselves having to fight with friends and family members about just "letting go."

The distance can become great between the griever and the friends and family members until that person has whittled down their support system to consist of little to no friends and the pain just gets worse. That was something Ma never warned me about. She never shared her pain at all. When I lost her, I experienced everything she struggled to accept, even though there were some things I still haven't accepted.

Mama Stories

I held onto my small social life and filled it with weekly parties, impromptu trips, and fine dining. My lush lifestyle was filled with lots of freedom, including the freedom to expand my financial resources to explore the unknown and more.

Musical Muse: "My Prerogative" *Song Lesson #3: I made this money, you didn't, right Ted? We outta here. Go see the world. You only have one life.*

When I agreed to participate to share my "Mama story," I wasn't exactly sure what I wanted to write about my mother. What I knew was that losing my mother drastically changed my life, but not before I learned lessons of love and relationships, independence and living life, pain, forgiveness, and regret. Because let's face it, if we can survive some of the most challenging times, surely we can learn how to take tragedy or trauma and learn from the lessons without becoming paralyzed by limiting beliefs. We are not our circumstance, and we are not our tough lessons taught by our moms. Realize that how we grieve can impact those we leave behind. Seek the help we may need. Learn how to break free and make it out, because they couldn't, and our legacy could depend on it.

As much as my mother made me angry, I loved her and felt her love for me ten times over. Hers was the type of love you feel deeply, even nine years after she has passed. Warm, forgiving, understanding, encouraging, supportive yet judgmental, overbearing, controlling, co-dependent.

If Ma were here today, my hopes would have been for her to read this book and see all the beauty that was within her. I would want her to see all the love that she left inside of me and those around her.

I would want her to see within this book how the music she shared with me throughout her life taught me lessons I plan to teach my daughter and my granddaughters. There are lessons that we must pass on and some curses we must break.

Payback's A B****!
VESTA JOI

Thanksgiving is one of my favorite holidays. It leads us to Christmas and the upcoming New Year's celebrations, and it is the day I yearn the most for the family togetherness and harmony. Thanksgiving weekend 2007 is by far one of the most memorable for me.

It went by too fast, another Thanksgiving weekend full of family fellowship had come to an end. In 2007, my daughters and I traveled to Atlanta to visit my Aunt Deloise and my cousins. It was such a good trip, and the food and fun did not disappoint. I took a deep breath in and let out a sigh while releasing the air in my lungs, exhaling the nostalgia of the weekend's memories and the time well spent.

The girls and I were about ten or fifteen minutes from our house in Charlotte, NC. My oldest daughter was always my navigator when we took trips to visit family. She sat in the front seat probably just as relieved to be close to arriving home as I was. My youngest daughter was in the back seat, she had slept most of the ride. Suddenly awake, she looked impatient and agitated. I figured she was ready to be home too. My youngest daughter's voice loudly interrupted our peaceful moment. She thrust herself toward the front seat and yelled, "I am about to be sick. This air freshener stinks. It's making me sick!" She grabbed the air freshener, ripped it from the rearview mirror and threw it out the back window.

"Pull over," she commanded. "I'm about to throw up."

I was in complete shock. I angrily swerved the car and pulled over onto the shoulder of the road. I put the car in park and turned my hazards on.

"What is wrong with you!" I said to my youngest daughter, as she opened the door, leaned out, and let what had been bottled up in her stomach erupt onto the graveled roadside. I gripped the steering wheel and watched her straighten back up and reach for something to wipe her mouth with. She stated the obvious, "I don't feel good."

As I pulled back into traffic my racing heart and thoughts were no longer the result of good memories of our beautiful Thanksgiving but of concern and confusion. I mentally recalled how she had had not been herself that entire weekend. She laid around like she wasn't feeling well the whole time, but not in a flu or cold-like way. I had a quick flashback of having just watched my daughter throw up and pull the top half of her body back into the car. My thoughts of the worst-case scenario robbed me of a sympathetic reaction. Fear and frustration gripped my soul and I yelled, "What the hell? What is wrong with you?"

"It must be something I ate." she said

"We ate what you ate and *we're* not sick!" Before she could say anything else, I yelled, "Are you pregnant!?" My mother's intuition had already answered the question.

"I don't know." she timidly responded.

Furious, my tone changed from yelling to screaming. I rapidly hurled questions at her.

"What do you mean you don't know? Are you having sex?" She was silent.

"Did you use protection?" I asked.

"I might be." She said quietly, my question answered.

I swallowed hard, took a deep breath, and said "Well, we are going to find out today!"

The tension in the car was thick enough to cut with a knife and the silence was even louder for the remainder of our five-minute drive home. We arrived home a little after 1 p.m. and my oldest daughter had not said a word. We all exited the vehicle solemnly, grabbed our bags, and headed into the house. I rushed to the kitchen and picked up the phone book, my fingers rustled through the pages to look up the number to Planned Parenthood. A home pregnancy test wouldn't cut it. We would need official documentation to receive any type of services or support. When I spoke with the staff person at Planned Parenthood, they said we could do a walk-in appointment.

The quiet 15-minute drive to Planned Parenthood felt surreal, my heart was still in my stomach. We arrived, filled out the paperwork and she returned with the nurse almost immediately. Her pregnancy test was positive, and the paperwork she carried confirmed her pregnancy and the due date of July, a little less than 8 months away. I wish I could say health and safety were my biggest fears for both of my daughters, but I feared teen pregnancy more. I looked at my daughter. My biggest fear as a mother was now a reality for the 16-year-old whom I'd had at sixteen. She was going to become a teen mother like I had been and like my mother before me.

All I could think about on the ride home was, *what did I do wrong?* I had tried to do things differently with my girls, different than my mom had done with me. I raised them in church, I put them in cheerleading and basketball; hell, I was even a volunteer coach for both sports. I told them about how hard it was for me growing up and raising children as a teen mom. I felt like such a failure as a parent in that moment.

We arrived home and I went into my room, closed the door, and began to cry. The thoughts and tears continued like drops of water from a leaky faucet. *I shouldn't have moved the girls from Youngstown, Ohio after all, it was the only life they had ever known with their stepfather, grandparents, friends, and community since they were two and three years old.* Youngstown was a nightmare for me, I was going to either lose my life or end up doing a life sentence if we had stayed there. Youngstown was a cycle of drama and misfortune. I knew if I wanted to live a peaceful and progressive life, I had to start over again in a bigger city. Moving was not an easy decision, it was a choice based on survival instincts. I had to leave my sons behind with my ex-husband and his crazy and vindictive new wife. I knew Charlotte as a city of refuge after visiting my high school best friend during spring break in 2004. It felt like home, away from my traumatic childhood. I can recall some good years in the south and Charlotte reminded me of that time. Life in Charlotte was my chance at creating a more prosperous life for my daughters and sons even if it meant only spending summers and holidays with the boys.

It had been two years and I was already working at Charlotte's only HBCU. We were living in a nice home and traveling to Ohio regularly since I missed the boys so much. Apparently uprooting two teenage girls from the only life they knew was the worst thing I could have done to them and our relationship. I snapped out of my thoughts, I needed to talk to someone and get some advice and comfort.

The first person most people want to call when they are in crisis is their mom. I wanted to turn to her even though for as long as I can remember, my mother and I had a strained relationship and had been at odds with one another. My mother's often narcissistic style of parenting led to emotional, verbal and physical abuse towards me. Despite all of that, I still needed and wanted my "mommy." My mom lived in Honolulu so it was not like she could rush to my home, or I could go to hers and get a hug or chat over a cup of tea. The minimum I expected from her was some sympathy, positive words of encouragement, and maybe some advice. I think I even desired a little excitement from her that she was going to be a great-grandmother because underneath my fear and sadness, I felt a tiny bit of joy about becoming a grandmother.

I picked up the phone and called her. She answered.

"Hey mom," I said, attempting an upbeat tone.

"Hey Passion," she said, using my childhood nickname as she often did. "How are you doing?"

My calm tone dissolved after hearing her voice. Sobbing, I said, "Your youngest granddaughter is pregnant."

"I can't understand what you are saying while you are crying," she said, as if my tears irritated her. "What happened?"

I took a deep breath and repeated, "Your youngest granddaughter is pregnant. I can't believe it. I tried so hard to prevent this from happening."

On the other end, there was complete silence. I waited. Why wasn't she saying anything?

"Well first of all, congratulations." I remember feeling somewhat comforted. Then before I could respond she stuck a verbal dagger in my heart and said, "Payback's a bitch, isn't it?" Her indignant tone surprised me.

I could not believe my ears. My heartache moved from my stomach to my head. I mumbled "WOW" and hung up the phone. She was good at making me feel worse than I already did about the things that went bad or wrong in my life. My mom had a way of adding a sprinkle of shame, a dash of blame, and an ounce of judgement to my toughest life experiences.

Did she really think I was being paid back for becoming a teen mother? Had she forgotten that I was molested as a child and that she had been a neglectful and abusive parent for most of my life adding to my childhood trauma? I made most of my bad choices as a pre-teen and teenager because I felt like I never had her attention and affection. I felt like the unlovable outcast middle child for as long as I could remember.

Did the woman who gave me life and who was supposed to shower me with love, kindness, and support just make this about her once again? According to my mother's statement, I had brought it upon myself. Did she feel that she purposefully got pregnant and had my brother at seventeen to pay her single father and deceased mother back?

My mother's hypocritical and hypercritical response hurt. I laid on my bed crying even harder after hanging up on her. I called my sister and told her that her youngest niece was pregnant and how our mom acted.

My sister said, "It's going to be okay." She was living in Honolulu and had moved there in 2006 to be with our mother given the heart problems she had developed due to her long battle with lupus. My sister did her best to console and encourage me.

"You will get through this," she said. "It could be worse." I hung up with my sister and felt a little better. I took some Tylenol P.M. and drifted off to sleep.

When I woke up, it was late in the evening. I needed to eat but did not have an appetite. I still could not face the girls, so I stayed in the room. My mind went back to the spring of 1991, in Newport, Rhode Island and the day I found out I was pregnant again at sixteen years old. My oldest daughter was maybe six months old, and I was dating my youngest daughter's dad and living with my mother at the time. That morning I drank some grapefruit juice and hives broke out all over my body. My mom took me to the emergency room and they said I had an allergic reaction to the citrus in the grapefruit juice as it was all I had consumed that day. The doctor also did a routine pregnancy test and informed me, in front of my mother and my then-boyfriend, that I was pregnant.

I was in total shock, my boyfriend was very happy, and my mother rolled her eyes in disgust. I remember that day vividly because I really did not want to be a teen mom with two children. I was fearful of having a child with my boyfriend, who was several years older than me, because he had started to become verbally and physically abusive. When we got home, my mother sat us down and told me I could no longer live at her home. She told me I would need to figure something out because she was not going to house and take care of me and two children. I started crying and my boyfriend consoled me and stated we'd figure it out. Several months later I became an emancipated adult and moved into my first residence as a teen mom which was in public housing.

Thinking about that experience made me feel determined to do whatever it took to prevent my daughter from having another child in her teens. Yes, I had failed to prevent my daughter from getting pregnant, but I refused to be unsupportive and unloving like my mother had been to me. I was going to be a supportive mother and a fantastic grandmother.

I got up from my bed and went to my daughter's room and told her that we were going to get through it together and that everything would be alright.

Christmas and New Year's Eve had passed, and it had been several months since I talked to my mother. My daughter was in her first trimester. We were adjusting and getting prepared for the new baby. My daughter transferred to the local alternative school where they had support for pregnant and teen parents, and she was getting government assistance for the prenatal care and benefits for her and her unborn baby. I felt a desire to call my mother and let bygones be bygones. I called my mother's home phone number and my stepfather answered. In a very frantic tone, he told me that my mother had been coughing very badly and had suddenly stopped breathing. He stated he had called the ambulance and had to go. I was so scared and felt in my heart that this time we were going to lose her. My sister and mother were barely communicating because of a disagreement they had around the Christmas holiday. I called my sister and asked her if she knew what was going on with Mom and she said no. I told her what our stepfather said, and she said she would call him.

My mother was admitted to the hospital for congestive heart failure on January 13, 2008. She was removed from life support and passed away on January 17, 2008. My mother's last words to me were "Payback's a bitch!" She never got to meet her first-born great grandson who came six months later. My biggest regret is that we never reconciled our turbulent relationship although there were numerous pride-filled and painful failed attempts made on both our parts throughout the years.

I look back and realize now that our family may not have broken the generational cycle of teen pregnancy. My siblings and I were all teen parents; however, my daughter is the only teen parent of my four children, which, in my mind, represents great success. I enjoy being a grandmother to my four amazing grandsons whom I love dearly. I often joke that no matter how much money I have to my name, I am always "four GRAND" richer.

As I reflect on my own mistakes and successes, I recognize my mother had her own childhood trauma coupled with her lupus battle and the unspoken struggles she surely must have faced during her fifty-two years of life. Over the years, I have learned that generational dysfunction and trauma can be transferred from parent to child, creating cycles of toxic behaviors and negative choices.

Many people refer to these repetitious patterns in families as generational curses. People discuss generational curses like some deep spell conjured up by a higher power or divine author who has decided who gets sickness, who gets health, who gets poverty, who gets wealth, who gets the good life, and who gets the bad life. I choose to reject the term because it is harmful and robs us of our power to choose a different path. I believe we should replace the phrase with generational cycles. Continuing generational cycles might be inevitable. However, I have found that such cycles can be survivable.

I am a survivor, and I am excited to share my story of resilience. This is the first of a series of stories I am working on, chronicling my survivor's journey and the determination it has taken to overcome generational cycles of trauma, drama, and dysfunction in my own life.

A Love Beyond Time and Space
KANDACE GRANT

My Mom came to visit me in a dream a few nights after she made her transition.

I was standing just outside of the boarding platform of a train station, kind of like the landing of the metro system in Washington, D.C. It was an exceptionally clear day with full-bodied clouds shaped like giant mounds of fluffy white frosting sailing across an incredibly vivid sapphire blue sky. The sun posed proudly in the middle of the brilliant portrait, smiling down on the glowing white train station and the sea of passengers flooding the platform below.

I stood captivated by the beautiful scene when I saw Mom emerge from the bustling crowd. As she walked towards me, I could see that she was wearing the same beautiful ruby colored African dress that she wore in our last family portrait, her locs flowing down her back and bound together by a matching sash wound around the top of her head. Even in my sleep, I felt pure joy surging through me.

"Mom??" I said almost breathlessly; then yelling, "Mom!!!"

I could see her so clearly, and I knew that she had come just to see me. Her mouth was moving, but for some reason, she didn't speak. Instead, she looked deeply into my eyes, and while holding up her cell phone, she pointed repeatedly to the screen repeatedly while shaking her head.

In that moment, I innately knew that all the text messages from Mom, which had mysteriously disappeared the day she died, would not be retrieved.

Both my daughter and my Aunt Freda told me in separate conversations that my mother had come to tell me that the messages were gone and didn't matter.

"Your Mother erased those messages somehow," Aunt Freda assured me.

"She knows her daughter, and she does not want you rehashing every conversation and looking back over things in sadness."

My daughter Risi agreed. "The messages don't matter, Mom. Mina (Risi's nickname for my mom since she was two years old) does not want you to worry about them. They are not your relationship, and they are not what she wants you to hold on to.

As I reflected on their words and on Mom's visit, I knew they were right. They had to be. It was the only explanation for why the many messages that she had shared over the years were the only ones missing from my phone; and, that they all disappeared on the very day she died. Even after extensive research between several departments, no one at the phone company could retrieve or even explain why the texts disappeared.

Gone! All the old photos and records of ancestors; all the personal recipes she perfected and shared; the genealogical research she had been collecting over the years; her pride-filled messages about our three children, my brother Kevin, my husband Keith, and me; her check-ins and random articles that she thought we'd like; and yes, even messages from her fussin' at me when I had stepped on her last nerve.

As I obey my mother's message to let go of those precious things, cleverly hidden clues in her visit unmask themselves, showing what she wants for me and my family. She wants me to fully appreciate the beauty of each moment, just as I did while standing in that dream scene. She wants us all to have the same joy, lightness of heart, and the almost tangible warmth that I felt when I saw her. She wants our family to continue nurturing the love of self and the pride in our mighty ancestry that she so carefully planted within us, which may be why she appeared in her regal, authentic African ensemble. Perhaps most importantly, she wants us all to trust that there is an unbreakable connection keeping all of us together no matter where we are, as her visit clearly showed.

There is even a message in where she chose to meet. Train stations represent new journeys, beginnings and endings, hellos and goodbyes. Perhaps our meeting was a goodbye of sorts, but Mom wanted us to know that she has only left her earthly form. She wants to reassure us that she is moving forward on her new journey, and that all is well.

I hear you, Mom. Even as I type these words, a choir of cardinals (our shared symbols for divine confirmation) are chirping their amens from the thick grove of trees in our backyard, one of Mom's favorite places. Leaves began to wave as the wind blew a strangely cool breeze for the usually steamier month of June, which caused my silver wind chimes to join the bird's song. Windchimes were one of Mom's favorite things too. Their sharp melody becomes the perfect background to a moving collage of memories about my first teacher, role model, and friend.

This is a story about my mom.

I splashed into this world in the early morning hours of December 7, 1970, in a little ranch style house in Columbia, South Carolina. Yes, I said splashed. I was born in the toilet.

You see, my mother was told, by many well-intentioned people, that she would know when I was coming because she would feel intense pain, so she waited for that to be her signal. Instead, she felt only a small cramp as she slept, and thought it must be gas. She woke up, headed to the restroom, and sat down. I fell out immediately, plunging into the water beneath her. In shock, she lifted me out of the commode before nearly passing out. My father, who had been sleeping, heard the commotion, and came into the tiny bathroom to find my mother on the now fluid-covered floor with me in her arms.

He yelled for my great-grandmother Viola, who had come to stay with them since I was due at any time. She calmly instructed my nearly hysterical father to call for an ambulance while carefully wrapping me in a blanket and gently rousing my mother as she helped cover her up. Grandma continued to tend to us both until the paramedics arrived and prepared us for our first road trip to the hospital.

A Love Beyond Time and Space

From our very beginning, Mom proved to be a woman of quiet strength who would give to her loved ones before herself. But who was this warrior woman, this powerful being that I have the honor of calling my mother?

My Mother was born Mildred June Hayes on August 23, 1950, in what she called a "tiny shack of a house" in rural Lexington, South Carolina. She hated her name.

"Millll-dred June?!" she would spit forcefully, her pretty face scrunched up as if she could taste the disgust, she had for it.

"All of my sisters have such beautiful names, and I got stuck with MILLL-dred June?!" she would scowl.

I always found it rather ironic that she so disliked what was actually a very fitting description of the woman that my mother was, at least at that time. The name Mildred means mild and gentle strength, and the name June means young. Gentle in both manner and speech, my mother was a beautiful, shy, intelligent young girl who hid behind thick, horn-rimmed glasses. Raised by her paternal grandparents, my mom lived just down the road from her parents and her eight younger siblings in a segregated neighborhood of shotgun houses in Columbia. The narrow, rectangular-shaped homes were built with all the rooms lined up directly behind each other without any hallways or restrooms to separate them. It was said, that if a bullet were shot from the front door, it would pass through the house and out the back door without hitting anything, hence the name.

Mom loved telling us stories about growing up in a poor, but close-knit community in the 1950's and 60's. It was a true village where the adults watched out for all the children as if they were their own. Elder Black women perched on front porches watching Mom and her peers as they walked home from school, yelling at those who dared to act out. It was an active hotline: news about anyone who had gotten in trouble at school would already have spread amongst the seniors by the time the kids arrived, so they could count on being chastised and possibly even spanked by neighborhood elders before they even got home. None of the adults played about getting an education, Mom would say. As Black people in an openly racist society, they understood its value, and had no tolerance for half-steppin'. They were personally invested in the children's success and taught with tough love. Despite societal conditions, substandard work and speech were not accepted; the bar was set high for all. For example, African American schools inherited the discarded textbooks and materials from local White schools. They were outdated and badly worn, often missing pages and barely legible, yet the teachers made the defective materials work, improvising when necessary.

When she wasn't in school or doing chores, most of Mom's childhood days were spent playing with her siblings and taking occasional rides to what she called "the country," meaning the outskirts of Columbia, where they would visit relatives, attend revival meetings, and stock up on meat from the farm. While young Mildred hated everything about the hog slaughters and seeing Grandma Viola and her sisters wringing chickens' necks for food, she thoroughly enjoyed the cultural ritual surrounding the revivals. All the old cars parked in the dense green wooded area just outside the old country white church, trunks packed with hot, freshly prepared meals and mouthwatering desserts proudly made and presented after

A Love Beyond Time and Space

services by church women who were just as serious about their worship as they were their food.

As a witness to life before and after desegregation, Mom always felt that segregation had its pluses, such as the strong sense of unity and entrepreneurial success that the Black community enjoyed. She taught us that desegregation was only intended to ensure equal access to what our tax dollars were already paying for, not to push us out of our communities.

She shared stories about the sad times too. The evil grip of racism suffocated much of their lives. One of the saddest stories was when Mom overheard her elders debating about Dr. King and the civil rights movement. While most of them welcomed the revolutionary changes, some were so badly traumatized that they didn't want him or any protesters in Columbia "stirring up all that trouble." My eyes still water with angry tears as I remember her repeating one older gentleman's resigned words: "At least they're not beating us anymore."

All those people, places, and the very time itself had a huge influence on my mother as she grew into a demure, sophisticated woman with the soft beauty so commonly attributed to Virgo women. Mom married our father a few years after high school, and she gave birth to me and my younger brother Kevin not long after. She was a devoted mother, pouring her very best into us. She filled our home with lots of books, home cooked meals, and learning. *Mom loved to cook and had a kitchen full of favorite recipes meticulously written in her beautiful handwriting.*

Mama Stories

Mom was attentive and empathetic: if we felt bad about anything—spoken or unspoken—she did too, and she went about trying to fix it. She believed in us, and it mattered to her that we believed in and cared for ourselves, one of the greatest gifts to us. She paid careful attention to what we liked, and often surprised us with things to make our childhood happy, such as baking our favorite desserts on Sundays.

Mom was a natural teacher, and she taught us both to read and write well before we even entered kindergarten. Using games, play, and casual conversations, she knew how to make learning fun. She eventually shared her passion for education with others, beginning as a substitute teacher before becoming a full-time staff member at St. Martin de Porres, Columbia's only Black Catholic congregation and school, where my brother Kevin and I were enrolled. There, Mom led small groups of children in reading and writing, tutored those needing extra help, and took it upon herself to help fellow parents to encourage learning at home. Like the teachers before her, it mattered to her that all children be empowered to learn, particularly Black children and children with special needs.

Her love of teaching was by no means limited to the classroom, however. An avid history buff, Mom brought people from the past to life by telling animated, colorful stories about their lives and experiences, complete with voices and vivid detail. One of her favorite stories to tell was the story of Harriet Tubman, her personal shero. She later went on to volunteer as a docent at Historic Columbia, where she led tours of Columbia's four historic homes from the early 19th- 20th centuries, including her favorite property, the Mann-Simons Cottage, which was a beautiful home owned by midwife Celia Mann, a formerly enslaved African who walked to freedom from Charleston to Columbia, South Carolina in 1850.

Mom was a spiritual person, teaching us by example how important it was to have a personal relationship with God. She was very generous and considerate of others. She took us to volunteer at the church's soup kitchen at least once a month to feed the homeless, and to personally deliver meals to poor families on holidays. As her daughter, she loved me enough to show me both her light and her shadow, always asking me to learn from what she called her mistakes. What I saw, however, was bravery and resilience, and I loved her even more.

Poised and articulate, Mom always carried herself with quiet dignity. I always admired her voice, which was beautiful whether she spoke or sang. I even loved the way she acted when someone made her angry. She never got loud or acted beneath herself. No, instead, she would make direct eye contact with the person and speak *very* slowly, enunciating her words with razor sharp precision as if she were talking to a two-year-old. Then, she would cut them with her icy, sarcastic, razor-sharp tone. Even if she was seething inside, she always appeared so composed that the other person never failed to look like an @$$hole!

As she grew older, Mom found her roar. She transformed, giving herself permission to shed things that no longer served her. She and my father divorced and she moved into her own apartment for the first time. She transitioned from her short, relaxed haircut to her thick natural hair, then eventually grew beautiful locs. She purchased a sporty new 1995 lilac-colored sports Saturn, and she even changed her name. She knew she had outgrown the quiet, just-keep-it-all-inside little girl born in that non-descript hut. The reserved Mildred June Hayes could not go where she was headed, so she was reborn as *Rukiya* Hayes, a Swahili name meaning *"she who rises,"* the perfect name for the woman who had begun to value her own growth.

While she remained a quiet person, Mom had a lot of personality. A fervent news watcher, she loved a good debate and would sometimes egg you on to provoke one. She was as funny and sarcastic as she was polished, so she loved comedian Katt Williams just as much as she loved listening to someone like renowned author Michael Eric Dyson. Because she could imitate anyone—accent and all—her stories about other people were animated and made you smile. She was much more open-minded than many of her peers, often defending equal rights for all, including gender equality.

Mom loved listening to everything from classic soul, gospel, jazz, and even reggae, and she loved spending time with our family. She loved hot cups of coffee (with extra cream and extra sugar) and ice-cold Pepsi, despite Kevin's reminders and my aggravating rants about how bad they were for rheumatoid arthritis or kidney disease which she'd been diagnosed with several years earlier. She found sacredness in nature, especially the ocean and the mountains.

Mom reconnected with her family just before she transitioned, leaving a powerful example of bravery and ancestral healing. She always told me that people do things in their own time. Mom was right.

I never know how to end a story, especially one like this. I almost don't want to. Writing this story and connecting with this writing circle has been such a beautiful, therapeutic way of viewing my mom and her continued journey.

Paule Marshall wrote, "Perhaps she was both child and woman, darkness and light, past and present, life and death—all the opposites contained and reconciled in her." This is my mom. The one who continues to transcend the earthly definition of death to visit with her family. The woman who gave birth to herself and became "the one who rises." The reserved personality whose bark became bite when defending children or those less fortunate. The refined lady in public who didn't mind cursing out a stupid @$$ politician on the news or an incompetent educator unwilling to use their power to make needed change for others. The woman who sometimes buried her own pain but insisted on healing ours. The faithful South Carolina native who swore that North Carolina's ketchup based barbeque was a sin, and who would take a Saturday morning drive with my brother to South Carolina just for the mustard-based barbeque and hash, but somehow still felt guilty about asking for a ride across town.

I am so very proud to be the daughter of such a worthy ancestor. I see her being embraced by divine love. I feel her presence.

This is the story of she who continues to rise; the woman bearing a love so strong that it transcends time and space.

Thank you, Mom. I love you

Taking Flight

MARY SANDERS

Simply put, I let it all go. I realized I had no control over much of anything; especially when it came to birth, death, life, or what happened within those parameters.

My mother had been diagnosed with early onset Alzheimer's a few years earlier, and as the disease picked apart the woman who birthed me at twenty-four; now some sixty years later, she sat fading before my eyes. It had become increasingly clear that her health was on a rapid decline and that she needed professional medical support because she could no longer be cared for in her own home. There was a stark contrast between the woman sitting slouched in an uncomfortable chair and the woman who always had some place to go and something to do.

I believe she was in her forties when she became a licensed driver after returning to South Carolina. She bought her first car and that car, like many of the others, was driven within inches of its automotive life and stranded by the roadside due to the tenacity of her driving. It seemed she was on a mission to make up for all the years of being transported by the Chicago Transit Authority. Pre-

Mama Stories

Alzheimer's, she visited others in nursing homes and hospitals. It was she who drove the more "seniored" seniors to community meetings, church services, and the grocery store. Her true passion was her beloved AME Zion Combined Choral Ensemble complete with an array of color coordinated outfits which were always conference ready. Absolutely nothing stood in the way of her going to rehearsals and performances...until the day she couldn't be found.

She sat sullen, silently winding her fingers together and staring so far off that it was pointless to try to keep her grounded in my presence. She could do little for herself and I certainly had no desire to weigh her down with all the unanswered questions still rattling around in my mind. It was not the time for forcing a bond that was severed over sixty years ago.

My mother, Mary Esther Lena Barnette, was born and grew up in a small South Carolina community. She was known as Maylena and everyone who knew her understood that she didn't take no mess. Maylena was outspoken and if anyone crossed her, she would tell folks straight to their faces what she thought. Shortly after my birth, I was told that my grandfather spent the first three months doing wellness checks on me and my mother. She was living in the city, seven miles from her home community, and the story goes that every day at the end of his workday, my grandfather drove to do his check-in and brought diapers and milk.

After the third month, he decided it would be better to take baby "me" to live with my grandmother, my aunt, two first cousins and him; so he did. I never heard my mother's version of the arrangement; she moved to Chicago without me. I did not see my mother again for years. I had no idea where Chicago was, or who

Maylena was. Perhaps she felt the same towards me. She never took the time to get to know me.

Why my grandparents did not call me by the name on my birth certificate, Mary Elizabeth, I never knew. I was called Deb in those early years. My grandparents never once called me Mary, neither did anyone else. Everyone unofficially adopted the name Deb. I guess the same way my grandparents unofficially adopted me.

I think I went by Deb in elementary school, too. However, by the time middle school came around, I became Mary. I really didn't care much for the name Deb. I am now realizing that the feeling of being unknown by family and, most importantly, unknown to myself relates to my sense of a loss of identity. I was often challenged and informed by others in the community about the comings and goings of my biological father. However, I noticed most of those supposed well-meaning folk struggled to keep their own indiscretions hidden.

Occasionally, letters arrived from my mother addressed to my grandmother, the contents filled with glossy photos of Maylena and her husband, and a steady stream of new babies posed in front of scenic backdrops with the envelope signed, *Mary*. I was a lover of books with a quiet curiosity that I nurtured creatively. I was always drawing and making things. I remember climbing into the backyard chinaberry tree, sitting on a branch with a book in hand, just taking it all in. None of Maylena's letters were ever addressed to me. I used to wonder if somewhere in the back of an old U. S. postal services vehicle, there was a pile of lost letters from my mother sent to Mary Elizabeth.

Mama Stories

My friend had invited me to travel with her to Chicago on a business trip. I happily accepted and secured my ticket months in advance. I was determined to make this trip happen, unlike the other failed attempts of a trip to Chicago. One time, I spent the money I had saved for my trip on a sofa which I adoringly named, "My Chicago Sofa" (just in case I never got there). Chicago had been calling my name for quite some time. Who knew that I would answer at such a critical turning point in my mother's life?

I wasn't going to cancel this time. Instead, I packed my bags, set them aside and prayed, "Lord please don't take her while I'm gone." I remember being dropped off at the airport and waving over my shoulder, but not looking back. I moved forward, knowing that I really wanted to be untethered for the moment. I didn't have any expectations or an agenda in mind, but intuitively I felt more connected to my mother as I boarded the plane headed to Chicago. She had never been the type to stand around waiting for anyone to tell her what to do. It was an opportunity I didn't want to pass up. Besides, there was nothing that I could do as my mother headed toward her final transition. I would just be standing around the dark halls of her assisted living facility, waiting for Medicare or Medicaid to respond and decide my mother's final residency status.

I recalled another time in my life when I was faced with a similar situation that I had absolutely no power to change. A wise and experienced woman said to me, "Mary, this is not about you." Those words helped me more than any other words that were offered during that painful and confusing time. I came to appreciate her wisdom and was able to apply it to my current situation. My mother's transition wasn't about me; it was about her journey with God. After much soul-searching, I decided not to cancel my trip and I prayed that if it was meant to be, I'd be back in time to say good-bye.

The day before I was scheduled to fly out was filled with anxiety amid the unanswered questions concerning my mother's long-term care and the dreadful prognosis. I checked in on her. Not much had changed. The best that I could do was to nurture my mother with kindness, acceptance, and love. I hadn't realized how much her absence had left a void in my life, even though there were many women who dearly loved me and cared deeply about me. I was surrounded by creative, vibrant, and interesting women at every stage of my life. However, I longed for and needed to be cradled, comforted, and nurtured by my mother.

After checking into the hotel, I stepped onto Michigan Avenue. The busyness of the streets had an electric buzz and I immediately felt the charge. I pulled my cell phone out and began creating my own scenic photo shoots posing in front of landmark buildings. I fell into rhythm like a native-born Chicagoan. I found myself walking faster and not looking up as much while becoming part of the movement of so many other people. My thoughts shifted to my mother. I wondered how it must have felt when she came to Chicago. She was young, free, and mostly unknown.

There were a few days that I spent sitting in the park, surrounded by life-sized art installations amidst homeless people sleeping on benches. Each day was an adventure and I felt free to come and go as I chose. Whether I sat for a few minutes, or walked through the streets, I imagined her life in Chicago. Did she blend in like I had, becoming a part of the fabric of people moving in all directions? Did she revel in the hustle and rush too as she learned how to navigate the big city streets? I felt her nudging me in a cosmic mother/child connection, the way nature created us. I resisted the urge to call home and check in with family about my mother's condition. There wasn't anything I could do. It was not up to me to figure anything out.

I sat beside sculptures in the park and wondered if she had ever visited that same space. I thought to myself, *I could have grown up here. Deep down I'm a country girl with a city heart.*

After the plane ride home, I was exhausted. I knew I needed to go and check on my mother to find out what was going on, but I was too tired. All I wanted to do was get a shower and take a nap. I woke up a few hours later just as the sun was setting. I went to visit the nursing facility and my mother's room. Thankfully, we were alone. The outline of her body on the bed was still and very frail, but my prayers had been answered--she was still with us.

I walked over and sat on the bed and leaned down very close to her face and whispered, "It's okay, it's okay. I'm not angry with you. I can see why you wanted to live in Chicago." I shared all that I could with her about the city and I reminded her of the excitement she must have felt when she first arrived in the Windy City. Deep within, I settled into a peace about not being there with her during my childhood, and believed she was at peace knowing.

I set the radio to a station playing soothing music. I looked into her eyes before I made my move to leave the room, I noticed one large tear slowly making its way from her eye to her cheek. I could have sealed it in a tiny bottle as a keepsake only to watch it evaporate. Instead, I collected it in my heart and set her free to take flight in peace.

Breathe

ANGELA M. HAIGLER

I sat on the couch in that room watching my mother breathe, in and out—with just an oxygen tube running through her nose. She seemed even smaller than I remembered. So tiny. Very warm. Breathing. The breathing. I imagined her lungs filling with fluid, without medication to keep them inflated. They had taken her off the machines when she was in ICU so her lungs were free to collapse. Relieved of her blood pressure medication and with no monitors, who knew what her blood pressure was? No food, except for what she might need "for comfort." They offered her ice cream and she forcefully shook her head, "no!" She did not want to eat, and she had lost her will to live—tired of fighting and ready to succumb...or was she? Had we made the right decision? I wanted to shout, "I take it back. No! Don't let her go. Keep her here no matter the cost or the toll it would take on her frail little body, not to mention the toll it would take on our family!"

She had been poked, prodded, pumped full of meds, but she wasn't improving. She was stable. Stable, but not thriving. The nurses in the

ICU were so pleasant. How could they keep up their positive expressions and conversations when they knew my mother was at a crossroads? How often had they seen this? Patients that won't eat amid monitors of all sorts blinking and making their steady, beeping sounds.

"She's not eating," they said. "What do you want to do?"

What do I want to do? I want her to start eating. She had been on an IV for several days, they said she needed to start eating, liquid food at least. I looked at her little face with the pillow of white hair framing her head. She would have hated having her hair like that, but it was difficult to preserve dignity in a hospital room. I wasn't worried about her hair; I just wanted her to eat. It was all new to me. At her previous hospital stays (and there had been many) my mother always ate. If she could start eating, she would gain weight and she could move to a regular room, and everything would return to normal.

Normal. When you have a parent with chronic illnesses, you know the drill. Hospital stay, treat the illness, go to rehab, go home and with help from home healthcare, your loved one is back to normal in weeks if not days. Surely, she'd get back to eating soon and we could get back on plan. Those five days are a blurry series of moments. I see everything. I remember it all. My foggy brain, the headache tapping at the back of my skull near my neck, me moving as if everything was going to get back to the regular routine. All Mom needed to do was start eating.

Breathe

The day before Valentine's Day, someone from the nursing home called my sister, Allison, who lived in Miami. They had rushed Mom to the hospital saying she'd had heart failure. Heart failure? My mom's heart had been her healthiest organ, far outpacing her lungs in terms of strength. This sounded serious and was something I knew that the daughter who lived the closest would need to handle. I didn't think twice. Although there were times in the past when I had to evaluate the urgency of one of Mom's crises, this was one of those times when I dropped everything and ran home to Mama. I knew I'd need some things, so I headed to my house, grabbed my overnight bag, threw some clothes in, and hit the road to Florence, South Carolina which was two and a half hours away from Charlotte, my home for the past twenty-seven years.

Mom's health had started declining after her COPD diagnosis in the Spring of 2009, when pollen traditionally begins to thicken the air, making breathing difficult. A heart attack alerted the doctors to a problem with her lungs. Technicians installed an oxygen-producing machine in her house, and she carried around a portable oxygen tank. Mom had such a strong spirit; nothing stopped her, and she didn't let COPD get in her way. She did everything she had always done; except with an oxygen tank on her arm.

There was crisis after crisis, with one of the scariest happening Thanksgiving weekend in 2013. My boyfriend at the time proposed to me with his mother, my sister Allison, brother-in-law, and nephew in tow. We celebrated the engagement, had a delicious dinner, and just enjoyed being around each other. The next day featured low-key family fun, but early Saturday morning, Mom appeared lethargic and wasn't herself. We called the paramedics and learned she'd contracted a rare strain of pneumonia that plagued the very young and the elderly and it was determined to take over her lungs.

The pneumonia turned septic, and after a miraculous sepsis protocol where she was given a 50/50 chance of survival, survive she did. I took a six-week leave of absence from my job to care for her as she was moved to a regular hospital room for several more days and received physical therapy at a local nursing home. Eventually, Mom bounced back. However, her memory wasn't as sharp. We later learned it was likely due to a mild form of dementia. I noticed little things, but I wasn't a doctor and not once did a doctor say that there could be neurological side-effects from anything that had transpired during or after the pneumonia and sepsis scare.

Audrey Tobiclaire Haigler Kirven neè Robinson, mother to Angela Marguerite and Allison Leslee, was a stubborn, strong-willed, loving human being. She had pulled through so many other situations, and I willed her to pull through again. I willed her to stay alive as I motored through small town North and South Carolina on that drive to Florence up Highway 15/401. With COVID protocols in place, it had been so difficult to see your loved ones. Mom had been languishing in a nursing home since November. There was no way to see her and no way to get real reports from the nursing home staff. I knew they were doing the best they could, but I felt powerless to be able to see for myself. I wanted to get my mom out of there so bad, but at least there, she was getting care and her meds. That's what I hoped, anyway.

I lost track of how many days I had been in Florence before they informed me that decisions would need to be made. I couldn't bring myself to sleep overnight in the ICU. My nerves were shot. A good night's rest was one gift I gave to myself. I had spent days, well into the evenings, there with her. But this time there were no quips, no conversations. No looks back and forth. When she was able to talk, I'd connect her with family members on face-to-face phone calls. I felt like the mother, grandmother, aunt, cousin and friend we all knew was in there, but there was no way to bring her out.

If we could just get her to eat. I remember hearing a weird rasping breathing sound coming from her that I hadn't heard before. *Where were her breathing treatments?* I got them started back up again and the next day the doctor spoke to me. He said that the sound I heard was food going into her breathing cavity. She wasn't swallowing properly. The breathing treatments weren't going to help with that.

"You are going to need to make some decisions," they told me. "Is there anyone to help with such things?"

They said Mom wasn't eating much, but when she was able to eat, the food spilled into her lungs, causing that rasping sound. The mechanism that diverted food to her esophagus was no longer working. That was a symptom of dementia. My positive outlook began to wane. How do we look on the bright side when your loved one's throat forgets how to swallow?

We had survived a heart attack, stents, lung issues, pneumonia, several chronic pain incidents, depression and more. Everything had been manageable. There wasn't a workaround for a throat that won't put food in the place it's supposed to go.

"Since she isn't eating, do you want to give her a feeding tube?" they asked. "Even with the tube," they warned, "There is a chance her saliva will still get into the lungs."

I checked my own swallowing function. Miraculously, my food and saliva knew what to do without me thinking about it. *How do you fix saliva dripping into the lungs?* One by one, each opportunity for Mom to have a routine recovery slipped away like in the game "Jenga." Each time we removed a block, the structure wobbled, but remained sturdy. Now it felt like the whole temple was about to fall and there was nothing we could do about it.

The tube meant surgery and giving Mom a liquid mixture of food through an opening in her body. She had left no advance directive--she never told us what she wanted. Would the woman who loved to eat want to eat that way? It broke my heart to think of her having to endure more poking and prodding on her body. It felt so cruel with a very dim outcome. I knew I wouldn't want that. Would she?

"Yes, there is someone," I said. "My sister who lives in Miami."

I called my sister and she headed to Florence as quickly as she could. I also called relatives and friends. What would Mom want? Would she want to get pumped full of liquid? Would she want a tube stuck down her throat? Nobody knew.

Remembering the conversation between my sister, the palliative care specialist and the doctor makes my ears throb to this day. I don't know if I truly understood that if we said no to the feeding tube, we were saying yes to hospice care and yes to our mother's death. I'm sure I heard it, but my ears were tired and not much was going in. My eyes were open, yet I couldn't see clearly. The pain at the base of my head kept knocking against my neck. When they talked about hospice, they made sure to insert the stories of people who sometimes came away from hospice and made it back to the hospital.

Hospice care was included in Mom's Medicare benefits, but continuing to keep her alive by any means necessary was not. I was struck by the very real issues of health care in this country. The rich don't have the same pressures as those with less wealth. Does their wealth make them more worthy of certain considerations? My mother had worked her entire life and when it came to critical decisions like the one we faced, her options were limited.

I had just started a new job and had begun a business on the side. What I needed was flexibility with decent pay. I didn't have either. When my job learned I couldn't get back right away, they let me go. My sister had a family in Miami with her own priorities and concerns. We were doing the best we could. I wanted Mom to come live with me, but at that time I was afraid she wasn't ready to give up her independence.

Overall, I feel there's little concern for the elderly today. United States policies are not elder-friendly. My mother had children to look after her, but what about those who don't? I believe being kind to the elderly through laws and policies would make the world a better place for everyone. These days, people seem concerned only about themselves and their interests, not seeming to realize we are interconnected. We all need each other for optimum survival. All those thoughts flew around inside my brain as my sister and I made the best decisions we could.

As they described the options, I could only think about wanting to bring my mother home--back to her house. I wanted to give her a chance for things to click back in. She would be back around the beautifully designed house she created amongst the things she painstakingly curated. She could take care of the plants that were dying without her care, in her own, familiar environment. I began thinking about how to get her home--maybe I could move to Florence temporarily. That's when my sister grabbed my hand.

"Angela," she said. "You have been there for Mom. You have driven her across the country. You took her to her fiftieth graduation anniversary at Morgan State. You took her to Dorian's wedding in Nashville. You have been a good daughter. Maybe it's time for you to let the experts take care of mom and you can focus on being a daughter again."

I looked at my sister's hand on mine. I looked over at the palliative care nurse with her caring expression and calm tones. I glanced at my mother's bed. The machines and monitors were in between us. She moved around, restlessly. It seemed to me like she was trying to talk. It was as if she knew we were talking about her. I know she wouldn't want us to argue. The doctor told us it was another sign of her worsening condition. I'm not sure I believed him but I felt a little outnumbered.

The tears that filled my eyes seemed to comfort me as they spilled over. Was it time for me to give in, too? Had we arrived at the situation Mom couldn't recover from? Sometimes I wonder what would have happened if we had given her the feeding tube. Would she have gained weight, recovered, proved everyone wrong once again? If I'd had a more stable job, been able to take off for six weeks with pay, maybe the result would have been different. What did the doctors know? All they had were years of experience and a handful of symptoms. They didn't know the fighter that was Audrey T.

Their advice and our instincts were all we had. Where do people go for these second opinions? Mom loved McCleod Hospital. She wouldn't want to go anywhere else. We decided. We would move her to McCleod's Health's hospice facility. Once the decision was made, everything happened so quickly. We were given a hospice information packet and the medical staff prepared Mom for the ten-minute drive to the hospice house.

The McCleod Hospice House was a beautiful facility. Aside from having to check in as visitors do at a hospital, it truly looked and felt like a home away from home. From the street, it resembled a house. Inside, the patient rooms were spacious, each with a hospital bed, a reclining chair and two guest chairs as well as a couch that converted into a bed for a guest wishing to spend the night. There was a sitting room with a fireplace and a library of books for patients and their families, but due to COVID restrictions, that space could no longer be used for group gatherings.

That damn COVID. I blame COVID for robbing me of my mother. Not because she had the disease, but because I'm convinced had there been no COVID, family and friends could have visited Mom in the nursing home while she recovered. They would have kept her grounded and my mother might be alive today. But thanks to COVID, since October 2020, Mom hadn't been home. She had left the hospital from a crisis and went straight to a nursing home for rehab to get stronger, but unlike the hospital, no visitors were allowed--not even one. There was no way to connect, except by cell phone, and she could barely use the cell phone. Sometimes she figured out how to call me or my sister, but those conversations varied with her grasp of reality.

Sometimes she saw puppies. Once she was worried about the insurance. Another time she told me she had to go to work, but she hadn't worked in years. Yes, if not for COVID, maybe we could have seen firsthand how she was doing, been able to ask questions. It was as if the dementia was moving faster than we could make plans. I just wanted to get her home, away from the facility. I wanted the chance to bathe her, change her, make sure she knew she was loved.

Should I have brought her home then? The doctor said I'd be in for a struggle. She needed 24-hour care. She'd have good and bad days. So, could I do that? Should I choose South Carolina or North Carolina? Allison, often the voice of reason I didn't want to hear, felt the nursing home was the best place for Mom, but she wasn't getting any stronger there. The dementia had taken over her mind and now it wanted her body.

Dementia had won. She'd struggle no more. I searched inside for my faith to take over. There was no turning back now. Without her medication, without food, she wouldn't survive. It was between my mother and God to decide when his tired daughter would come home. I slept on the couch every night she was there until she passed away on February 27, 2021, at 1 a.m. I lay right next to her on the hospital bed. Seated in the chairs and couch in the room were Allison and my brother-in-law, along with our play brother, William, who has been like a brother to us and a son to Mom. Mom waited until Allison and I drifted off to sleep to begin her journey. They say the dying often do that. Our "brother" William woke us up. We were blessed to see her take her last breath and we prayed over her departed spirit.

Losing her has been one of the toughest things I've ever had to endure. Every year it gets a little bit better and a little bit worse. I'm so grateful to have had Audrey Tobiclaire Haigler Kirven neè Robinson as my mother. Our relationship was the motivation for the creation of this anthology. Through The Mama Stories Writing Project and my life, I pray that I can be an acceptable representative of the legacy her life embodied.

About The Authors

Mama Stories

AMY COTTON

Originally from Anderson, Indiana, Amy Cotton is a teacher in Charlotte Mecklenburg Schools residing in Charlotte. She studied at Bethune-Cookman University. The mother of one son, she says, "At the end of the day it's great to come home to your family and know that God has truly blessed you."

KIRSTEN USSERY

A Hickory native currently residing Charlotte, NC, Kirsten started her career in Charlotte interning with the Charlotte Chamber of Commerce and Duke Energy. She then lived and worked for more than 20 years in Detroit, Michigan. Kirsten has been a speaker on various panels about entrepreneurship including the Small Giants Conference, Net Impact Food Panel and JPMorgan Chase's CityLab Detroit Global Summit. She is a graduate of the Goldman Sachs 10K Small Business Program. With over 20 years combined experience in both communication/public relations and the food industry, Kirsten is a veteran in research, management, operations, communications, and marketing.

LUCY A. SAMS

Lucy is a Serialpreneur, and the current Owner of SuperBig SB Adventures, a children's book publishing company. She has spent over 15 years in the "World of Writing," contributing with bylines and titles for travel articles, children's books, community advocacy pieces, and a catalog of ghostwriting contributions. A sample of her work can be found on her blog; Suavexor.com. She dedicates her time to being of service to her community, globetrotting, and enjoying the people she loves. Her motto is "There is ALWAYS a way."

TANNY SWAN

Tanny is a native of Chicago, Illinois, and has also called Michigan, Georgia, and Iowa home. A high school English teacher for over twenty years, she has helped hundreds of students discover a love for literature and writing. Having earned graduate degrees in both English and Educational Leadership, she finally chose to follow her heart and pick up her pen. This essay marks her debut as a published author, and she is cheered on by her husband, Cliff, and her two daughters, Sydney and Nia. When Tanny isn't reading one of her many unfinished journals, she can be found eating chips with guacamole, planning her next vacation, and thinking about way too many things at once. She is a member of Delta Sigma Theta Sorority, Inc. and the owner of Tanny Swan Productions, a very small business devoted to producing opportunities for others to become the very best versions of themselves.

TOMI BANKS

Tomi is a serial entrepreneur and originator who loves to create. She is the founder of T. Banks Creative, a Branding Media Boutique that offers a one stop shop for business branding, graphic design, photography, and social media management. She has combined her talents of creativity and speaking to motivate women in various arenas. Tomi delved further in encouraging her Sisters when she became an Amazon Best Selling Author with her book: *Finding A Path To Victory* where she and nine other authors boldly demonstrated resilient courage and achievement to help others.

Tomi Banks earned her B.A. in English Literature and her Master of Education in Communications Disorders from North Carolina Central University. She also received her certification in Event Design from the University of North Carolina Charlotte. Tomi believes that God created us all to be a masterpiece. By serving through her creativity, she helps others enhance their canvas.

RITA SAMUELS

Rita is a working professional and educator in Clover, South Carolina and a dedicated "Boy Mom." She is a graduate of Winthrop University and Francis Marion University. Her happy place is a beach. She is a fan of writing, education, and travel.

MONICA BROWN NASH

Monica grew up on the south side of Chicago where she began her love affair with words. In her Junior year at South Shore, she entered a poem that was selected for publication in the *Creative Writing* Magazine. That began her love of expressing herself through poetry and short stories. While in high school her parents moved the family to Tuscaloosa Alabama, returning to Chicago for her senior year. Monica attended the University of Georgia but obtained her BA degree from DePaul University in Chicago. As a young adult, Monica moved to the Bay Area where she lived for 14 years. There she met and married her husband and best friend Kim. They now reside in Arlington, Texas. Monica enjoys reading, writing, traveling abroad with Kim, and weekend getaways with girlfriends. Monica continues to write words of encouragement to family members and friends which she hopes to publish one day.

About The Authors

TIFFANY GRANTHAM

Tiffany is a native of North Carolina and works as a Librarian Assistant. She is an alumna of North Carolina A&T State University and received her M.F.A in Writing from Lindenwood University, which further encouraged her appreciation of the written language and community. She is currently pursuing a bachelor's degree in music interdisciplinary studies from Berklee College to merge her two loves: music and literature. When not reading or writing, Tiffany is growing her in-home library and caring for her plant babies, Goldie, Zora, and Wisdom. *The Mama's Story Writing Project* is her second appearance in an anthology.

YAYA S.

Meet Yaya S., a dynamic and adventurous Johnson C. Smith University alumna, who has a passion for nature and a zest for life. As a mother of two and a proud grandmother of three, she is lovingly known as Yaya to her precious grandkids. Yaya S. is not only a successful Business Strategist but is also a true adventurer at heart. You can often find her hiking along beautiful trails, chasing waterfalls, or trying out exciting outdoor activities. With her unique blend of creativity, determination, and passion for adventure, Yaya S. is a true inspiration to all who know her. Her first piece in our collaborative book is sure to be a hit. Hold on tight and get ready for an adventurous ride as Yaya S. takes you on a journey of self-discovery and exploration.

Mama Stories

VESTA JOI

Vesta is the mother of four adult children and four grandchildren. She earned her Bachelor of Arts degree in Business Management from Belmont Abbey College in Belmont, NC. Prior to that, she earned her Associate's degree in Information Technology from Youngstown State University in Youngstown, OH. In her leisure time, Vesta enjoys fun activities with her family and friends, writing, reading, traveling, and participating in community outreach/engagement opportunities, and attending cultural enrichment events. Vesta hopes to continue to write stories that encourage individual and family health and wellbeing. Her piece, "Payback's a B***H explores the generational loop of transferred trauma when a woman attempts to break generational curses and life limiting behavior. Her story is one of tragedy, triumph and transformation. As the first in her family to attend and graduate from college, Vesta lives in Charlotte, North Carolina.

KANDACE GRANT

Kandace is an author, advocate, writer, and speaker. Her first book, *Be Willing! How to Live an Affirmative and Empowering Life Right Now*, is an inspiring guide to getting up again after being blindsided by a sudden detour. Kandace is a proud wife and mother of three amazing young adults-- including her youngest son who was diagnosed with autism, epilepsy, and eventually kidney disease before suddenly passing away at the age of 24. Kandice advocates for and speaks to fellow parents/caregivers of children diagnosed with special health needs in her son's honor. A grateful kidney transplant recipient, she does the same for kidney health and organ transplantation as a National Kidney Foundation Kidney Educator and as an Ambassador for LifeShare of the Carolinas. Kandace graduated from the University of South Carolina with a degree in Journalism. Her work has appeared in Charlotte's *Pride Magazine* as well as in well-known state and regional nonprofit publications.

MARY SANDERS

Mary was born in Rock Hill, SC; she is the proud mother of two wonderful human beings. Her artistic interest was apparent at a young age and supported by her adoring grandfather who allowed her to paint embellishments on the walls of her bedroom. Mary is a self-taught artist who learned many crafting techniques from her eclectic aunts and grandmother. As an adult, she studied art at Winthrop University. She credits her explorative nature, love of stories and free flowing visual musing as the true inspiration of her work.

ANGELA M. HAIGLER

Angela is a marketing communications professional, journalist, freelance writer, and creative writing instructor. She holds a B.A. and M.S. in journalism and mass communication, and an M.F.A in creative writing. Her essays are featured in the anthologies, *The Image in the Mirror* and *Unspoken.* Her work can also be found in publications such as *CourierNewsroom.com*, *Beautiful Truths* literary magazine, *Library Journal*, *The Charlotte Observer*, *Change Seven* literary magazine and Charlotte's African American lifestyle magazine, *Pride* where she is the Book Reviewer. The recipient of a 2020 ASC Emerging Creator Fellowship, Angela empowers aspiring writers to pen their stories and share them with the world.

www.ingramcontent.com/pod-product-compliance
Lightning Source LLC
Chambersburg PA
CBHW050827160426
43192CB00010B/1930